Communication Land Mines!

18 COMMUNICATION CATASTROPHES AND HOW TO AVOID THEM

Marty Clarke

Publisher's Cataloging-in-Publication Data

Clarke, Marty.
Communication Land Mines! : 18 communication catastrophes and how to avoid them./ Marty Clarke.
p. cm.

ISBN 1-893095-19-3

1. Business.communication   2. Interpersonal
communication   I. Title.

Library of Congress Control Number: 2003101106

10 9 8 7 6 5 4 3 2 1

This book is dedicated to Tommy and Denny.

Acknowledgements

- Bil Holton edited. Tough to say how this would have looked without Bil.
- Alison Hodges proofread. There's a difference between a bear and a man in a bear suit. Alison's the bear. I'm very lucky to have her on my team.
- Cher Holton's design skills were the window through which a document passed into a book.
- Jane, Matthew, Katie, and Lucy showed quite a bit of patience. They are my family without whom none of this would have been possible or worthwhile.

As sincerely as I can I want to say thank you to these people for all their help throughout the development, creation and completion of this project.

Table of Contents

Preface

The Margin of Victory

In 2001, on Sunday, May 27th, a rookie driver named Helio Castroneves won the Indianapolis 500. Beyond the glory of winning one of the world's most prestigious races, Helio and his race team took home a purse of $1,270,475. Not bad for a Sunday.

Right behind him, arriving in second place was a driver named Gil de Ferran who took home a nifty $482,775. Gil and his team didn't lose by much. In fact, on that day, as is somewhat common at the Indy, a very slim margin separated first and second place.

On that day Helio Castroneves beat Gil de Ferran by a quick 1.7 seconds.

Let's do the math. By being 1.7 seconds faster, Helio earns $787,700 *more* than Gil de Ferran. Because they were 1.7 seconds slower, Gil de Ferran and his race team have to split roughly 62% *less* money than the Castroneves team.

The moral of the story is Castroneves did not have to be 62% faster than de Ferran to make 62% more money. He just had to be 1.7 seconds faster. Actually, he didn't even need to be *that* much faster. All Castroneves had to do, all any driver has to do, is set him or herself apart from the pack enough to be in front when the checkered flag drops. Helio did just that and he wound up in the winner's circle holding a trophy in one hand and a fat check in the other.

This book is about setting yourself apart from the pack. In the business arena, the margin of victory is often just as slim as it is in racing. And it is my conviction that the winners and losers in business are determined by who sets him or herself apart with superior communication skills.

Who gets the sale and who walks? Who gets the job and who gets turned away? Who gets the promotion? Who gets the raise?

You do.

You do if you can emerge as a superior communicator, capable of transmitting ideas and concepts in simple yet compelling ways, regardless of the medium. Do that and you *will* set yourself apart from your peers. You *will* get noticed.

But just like minor driving errors can lead to huge crashes on a race track, so can careless communication errors cause you serious professional damage. The trick is to avoid those communication errors that your peers and even your superiors keep making day after day. This book can help you do that.

Because if I can help you spot those errors, those communication land mines, and teach you a few ways to avoid them, then I can help you begin to stand out in the most powerful way possible. I can help you begin to form a communication skill set that will place you in whatever professional winner's circle you like.

A Few Details Before We Start

Who is Mr. Whizbang, and Why Does He or She Want You to Read This Book?

Who is Mr. Whizbang?

Simply put, Mr. Whizbang is anyone you are looking to impress with how well you communicate. Whatever your endeavor, Mr. Whizbang is the one who has the authority to make or break the success of your efforts. Mr. Whizbang is the person with true power. My experience has taught me that, in any business situation there are two distinct types of power: the power to recommend and the power to decide. Mr. Whizbang has the power to decide. Once you've gained an audience with him or her, you cannot afford to make a poor impression on Mr. Whizbang.

Mr. Whizbang is:

◆ Your prospect
◆ Your customer

- The CEO
- The CFO
- The CMO
- The C-Whatever
- Your boss
- The person on the other side of the desk
- The person who can hire you
- The person who can admit you to college
- The person who might donate a large check to your charity
- The person you hope will become a member of your professional association

You get the picture.

Whizbangs are everywhere. They are specific to no gender and no nationality. These folks are in positions of power, access, and authority. Most, but not all, tend to have status, sophistication, and sparkle. For some Whizbangs, the personal pronoun "I" is their coat of arms. All of them have healthy egos, well groomed opinions, and narrow agendas. Safe to say, you cannot afford to annoy Mr. Whizbang by stepping on communication land mines all over the place.

Mr. Whizbang is going to form his or her initial impression of you almost entirely on the basis of how you communicate. Stepping on a communication land mine is often fatal to that impression. The reason for this is Mr. Whizbang is going to form that opinion of you rather quickly, and he or she has neither the time nor inclination to groom you if that impression is negative. So if you come across looking like an amateur, Mr. Whizbang is going to see that right away and it is usually "game over" very quickly. It has been my experience that Mr. Whizbang is not the type of person who deliberates too long on anything. Decisiveness is a key element of Mr. Whizbang's personality and patience is not typically one of Mr. Whizbang's virtues. These traits are not born out of recklessness. They are born out of experience. Mr. Whizbang got to where he or she is because he or she got good at making these decisions quickly and Mr. Whizbang is right a whole lot more times than Mr. Whizbang is wrong.

Speed is key in Mr. Whizbang's world. Time is easily the most precious commodity and my experience has taught me that a large part of any approval decision on projects, purchases, and especially people—hiring them, firing them, or promoting them—is based on whether or not they are a waste of time.

So, in a world where decisions are being made and opinions are being formed with alarming speed, the trick is to avoid every communication land mine you can so you can emerge quickly in Mr. Whizbang's mind as a solid professional and certainly not a waste of time.

For the purposes of this book I will use the name "Mr. Whizbang" even when the person in the story is a woman. Also, in the case that there is actually someone out there named Mr. Whizbang who feels guilty by association, I can only say any relationship between the Whizbangs in this book and the Whizbang on that person's driver's license is entirely coincidental.

A word to the wise: As I have stated, there are a multitude of Mr. Whizbangs out there. However, there are many *more* people out there who either knowingly posture themselves as Mr. Whizbang or who actually think they *are* Mr. Whizbang, but they are unfortunately overestimating their own importance. It has been my experience that the latter is far more common than the former.

Here's a story to illustrate.

A relatively long time ago, a mid-size copier company ran into a bit of financial trouble. They had 23 sales offices along the East Coast, about 1,200 employees, and a nice big building for their headquarters in the South East. However, one day, when they looked around they found they had no money, only debts.

So they asked a venture capital firm in New York to give them an enormous amount of money to help them along. The New York firm complied and the copier company went on its way.

Now, keep in mind, when a New York VC firm (or pretty much anybody for that matter) gives you a significant amount of money, it is rare that they just give it to you and walk away. Typically, and certainly in this case, someone is appointed to watch very closely what you do with all that cash.

The story shifts now to a phone call I got from a friend who owns a large public relations firm here in my home town. We'll call him Mario. Mario wanted very much to make the copier company his newest client. This would be a client in the neighborhood of say 250 to 300K. Neato, huh?

Mario called me to see if I had any ideas on how to approach the Executive Management Team because he knew I was moderately familiar with them. It boiled down to "Who is Mr. Whizbang and how do I approach him or her?"

Mario: So what can you tell me?

Marty: There's a guy there named Alan.

Mario: Alan's the guy?

Marty: Alan is the CEO. Says it right on his door.

Mario: What's he like?

Marty: He rules with an iron fist. He's actually a lovely guy, but clearly he's the man over there.

Mario: Who's Alan got around him running things?

Marty: Um, well pretty much what you'd expect. He's got a money guy, an operations guy, a sales guy, and a legal guy. All the departments eventually report up to those four.

Mario: These all Executive VPs?

Marty: No clue, but with a company that size, it stands to reason.

Mario was most pleased and told me how he was going to write Alan a nice hand-written letter of introduction. I disagreed on this strategy entirely.

Mario: What? You just said Alan's the guy.

Marty: Alan's the CEO. And to the naked eye, Alan is Mr. Whizbang. Absolutely. This guy looks, acts, and is regarded by most people in that building as Mr. Whizbang. But even though Alan is the CEO, nothing could be further from the truth.

Mario: I'm lost.

Marty: You heard about how they got all that money from the New York VC right?

Mario: Absolutely.

Marty: Well if you want an audience with Alan, if you want Alan's undivided attention, my advice is to get your letter of introduction on the desk of the guy whom the New York firm appointed to keep a close eye on all that money. Alan doesn't blow his nose without checking with that guy first. That guy, Mario, is Mr. Whizbang. Believe it.

I happened to have had at that time, the New York guy's name and gave it happily to Mario.

I knew that Mario had exactly one shot to make a good impression on Mr. Whizbang in New York. If he nailed it, he might get recommended to Alan and then away we go. If he wasn't careful and stepped on a communications land mine, he was likely to blow his chance and go quickly into Mr. Whizbang's "pay you no mind" bucket from which there is rarely any escape.

See, that's what I'm talking about. That's why I wrote this book. Communication skills *count*. They count for a lot. The occasions to step on a land mine come pretty often in the business world. They pop up every day. The land mines are out there and in these days of fierce competition and information overload it is critical to set yourself apart by emerging as someone with excellent communication skills.

> *The information most useful to me... comes from quick, oftentimes casual exchanges. This usually reaches a manager much faster than anything else. The more timely the information, the more valuable it is.*
> – Andrew S. Grove, CEO of Intel Corp.

So anyway, I know you are dying to know... I'll tell you how it turned out with Mario, Alan, and Mr. Whizbang in New York.

I hung up with Mario, pleased to have done my buddy a good deed. That was a Tuesday. A scant ten days later I got a call from Mario who was overjoyed to tell me that he'd hand-written a nice letter of introduction and sent it to the New York guy. The New York guy apparently forwarded the letter to Alan with a note on it which read "Take a look at these guys."

Mario got a 7:45am call from Alan the next day. By the end of the next week, Mario and his team were to be front and center in Alan's private conference room with Alan,

Alan's Chief Marketing Officer, and Alan's Executive Vice President of Sales ready for a pitch meeting.

Game on.

Apparently, Mario's note made the right impression on Mr. Whizbang.

What if Mario had chosen a different route? What if it had been a phone call? A voice mail message? An e-mail message? Or a visit to the New York office?

Regardless of his choice, Mario's communication skills were going to have quite a bit to do with his success, or lack there of, with Mr. Whizbang. His first impression was going to be a lasting one. This impression was going to form the all important "go, no-go" in Mr. Whizbang's mind and all of this was going to come down to how well Mario was able to communicate.

Why Does Mr. Whizbang Want You to Read This Book?

It bears repeating that one of the most important things you need to keep in the very front of your mind is that Mr. Whizbang spends his or her life pressed for time. Any time a land mine goes off, time is wasted. Many of the communication land mines in this book have to do directly with the issue of time. By reading this book, and adopting a few ways to avoid some communication land mines, you can set yourself apart in Mr. Whizbang's eyes as someone who is a valuable contact and not someone who is going to waste his or her time.

If Mr. Whizbang could guarantee that every person with whom he or she dealt would be to the point and professional, why, he or she would love it. If Mr. Whizbang woke up one morning and at the foot of his or her bed a genie appeared and said, "No one will waste your time today," Mr. Whizbang would practically skip to work. Tripping communication land mines distracts Mr. Whizbang from the task at hand and is therefore a time waster. If you avoid the communication land mines, you will emerge in Mr. Whizbang's mind as a true pro, a valuable contact, and someone with whom it is a pleasure to do business.

Also, every business day Mr. Whizbang is inundated by would be vendors, job seekers, and the like. Everyone is vying for Mr. Whizbang's time. One side of Mr. Whizbang's head is saying "Ignore everyone! Keep doing what you're doing and get something done!" The other side of Mr. Whizbang's head is saying "We have to keep an eye out for the companies and people that can make a difference to us. We cannot afford to miss out!" And so, if you are one of the people for whom Mr. Whizbang makes some time whether it is on the phone, via e-mail, regular mail, or a face-to-face meeting, the need for you to stand out from the crowd is in both your interests.

That is why Mr. Whizbang wants you to read this book and soon I will wax philosophic about the importance of effective communication skills in an effort to help you differentiate yourself.

Why I am in a Unique Position to Wax Philosophic on These Matters

For the last eleven years I've spent time on both sides of the Mr. Whizbang's desk. I've been on both sides of that professional information exchange. I've been a job applicant, a sales person, a sales support person, a sales manager, and a marketing executive. This book is about what I observed or learned through trial and error about business communications throughout all that time.

Marty The Sales Guy: For seven years I sold, supported the sales of, and managed other people who sold, commercial long distance, data, and wireless products. I was the one making the cold calls, sending out the letters, and going on the appointments. And even though I was actually a pretty good sales and sales support person, I am convinced I made every mistake in there is and maybe even added a few no one had thought of before. Later, as a sales manager, I had a front row seat to watch my own reps step on communication land mines.

Marty The Marketing Guy: More recently, I spent four years as Vice President of Marketing for a regional telecommunications provider. No one told me this when I got the job, but when you get a VP title, your name immediately gets put on some list somewhere and subsequently, over time, every sales person in the galaxy calls you. So for those four years I was *receiving* the cold calls and sitting on the *buy* side of the desk during appointments. I should mention that the more calls I got and the more appointments I sat in on, the easier it got to spot the pros from the amateurs sitting across from me.

It was during my time as a marketing VP that the idea for this book occurred to me. I began to catalogue the communication land mines: The Instant Launch, The Endless Message… I kept a list of all of them and that list grew and grew until I identified, in my opinion, the definitive collection.

What did I observe over those years? What did I learn from my travels through a business landscape dotted with communication land mines?

Well, I'll tell you. After eleven years of experiencing pretty much every communication mistake out there, I have categorized eighteen of the most common and glaring land mines that business professionals have been stepping on with alarming regularity.

Business communication is a minefield to be sure. There are plenty of places to step poorly and find yourself on the outside looking in. But it doesn't have to be that way. I'd like to provide you with a road map of how to step *around* a few of the most common business communication catastrophes on your way to becoming a much more professional presence in your field and thus much more successful. This book is not only about identifying the communication land mines. It is also about avoiding them.

I've always felt very frustrated when I've checked my mental rearview mirror and see the communication mistakes I've made. The reason is because so many of the communication land mines I've stepped on were usually so *easy* to avoid if only I'd used a little foresight. If only I'd had these land mines pointed out to me I could have steered around them with almost no more effort than it took to jump on them. If only I'd read this book.

Frustrating in a completely different way were the times when I could see a land mine coming: when I was on the Whizbang side of the desk, or when I'd accompany a sales rep to an appointment or listen to a rep on the phone. Sometimes I'd see it off in the distance and it would be easy to coach a rep around it. But all too often were the times when I'd see the communication land mine only seconds before my rep or a vendor or a job applicant would set it off. This was especially true during face-to-face meetings.

There are two characteristics about almost all communication land mines that make them insidious:

1. The damage done by communication land mines is often silent and invisible.

Let's agree on a distinction. We are talking about *communication* land mines. There are real land mines and there are communication land mines. Apparently, in the case of setting off a real land mine, an actual explosive device, you are alerted almost immediately to the fact that you have triggered one. From what I gather, it's tough not to notice. Certainly I am *not* referring to those types of land mines.

In the case of communication land mines, the damage is unseen and unheard. How are you supposed to avoid something like that? If a bell went off any time you stepped on a communication land mine, the process of avoiding them would be easy. You would get adept at noticing the behaviors that led up to the bell-ringing incidents. But no bells go off when a communication land mine blows up.

Have you seen Robert Redford's movie *Jeremiah Johnson*? Go rent it. In a nutshell, Redford plays a soldier, disillusioned by his time in the Civil War, who decides to become a mountain man. This is easier said than done, but eventually he meets up with an old and very capable mountain man, "Bear Claw" Chris Lapp (played by Will Geer) who teaches him "the ways of the mountain" and in doing so saves Jeremiah's life.

One of the tricks "Bear Claw" shows Jeremiah is how to dig a little trench under your sleeping space and lay down some embers from the fire. Then you cover the embers with dirt, lie down on top of it and *voila*, you're warm all night.

Jeremiah tries this but in the middle of the night he jumps up with the back of his clothes smoking and nearly on fire.

"Bear Claw" looks over at him and says "Didn't put enough dirt down. Saw it right off."

It would have been nice for a bell to have gone off right as Jeremiah was putting an insufficient layer of dirt between himself and the embers. That would have saved him the pain of being scorched in his sleep.

Clearly, one of the messages the audience gets at the end of this scene is that "Bear Claw" could have helped Jeremiah out, but instead chose to let Jeremiah learn the lesson for himself so the lesson would be sure to stick. And as a manager, I used to do that too sometimes.

In the absence of communication land mine bells going off, how do we avoid them and the professional damage these land mines do?

The first thing you can do is be aware that they are out there. With this book in hand, you can begin to identify and recognize them. The second thing is foresight.

DEFINITION

foresee (transitive verb): to see (as a development) beforehand

Synonyms: anticipate; implies taking action about or responding to something before it happens

---

Aspire to attain great professional foresight and anticipation and you will soon find yourself emerging from the pack. No bell is going to go off. You have to see the communication land mine coming beforehand.

2. *Very few Communication land mines are "Deal Killers" in and of themselves*

This fact is both good news and bad news. The good news is obvious: if you step on a communication land mine, you may still achieve your end result whether that is a sale, donation, job, or whatever. The bad news is less evident. If you trigger a communication land mine Mr. Whizbang typically will not interrupt the situation to say:

Mr. Whizbang: Whoopsi! I'm sorry Marty. I'm afraid you've triggered the No Next Steps communication land mine. This means you have to leave my office immediately. We cannot do business together. Nothing personal, fare thee well and all that. But be a good boy now and scram.

One mistake does not a deal-killer make. But be advised, communication land mines add up. And if they do, their combined mass can cause enough damage to kill a deal. The challenge lies in the fact that you cannot see them adding up. Mr. Whizbang cannot see them either. Mr. Whizbang feels them. Mr. Whizbang has no secret ledger upon which he or she records your every effort, both good and bad. An opinion of you, a level of trust, a fondness or general distaste for you is all being calculated, added up subconsciously and sometimes consciously in Mr. Whizbang's head. And since you do not see your score as you go along, since you do not see the land mines adding up, it is easy to proceed merrily along not knowing you are digging a hole for yourself.

Let me relate this to a universal human experience. Besides a list of communication land mines, I keep a list of universal human experiences. So far I have two. The first universal human experience is Birth. Everyone has to be born. There are many variations on that theme but since none of them apply to this discussion we'll move swiftly to the second universal human experience on my list: the experience of opening your credit card statement at the end of the month and having your head explode owing to the unanticipated magnitude of your balance. The internal monologue usually goes something like this:

Poindexter: Oh man, the credit card bill. I bet this thing's gonna be like $350.

Poindexter: (Opens the statement.) AAAAHHH! $1,464.82? No way! Reporting error! Computer glitch! Theft! Can't be. Can't be. No way did I buy that much.

Poindexter: (Looks through the list of transactions.) Ok, that one's right. Dinner with Frieda at Le

Rondelle. Mountain bike. That's right too. DVD player. Plane tickets...

On and on Poindexter goes. He never saw it all add up. And now he's in a hole. Communication land mines are quite a bit like that. They add up in Mr. Whizbang's mind. Adding insult to injury, Mr. Whizbang very rarely delivers you your "statement." Most times when business situations fall apart you never do know quite why they did. All you know is that you did not get what you wanted and the hole resembles a professional grave.

As I have stated, communication land mines add up quietly over time in Mr. Whizbang's head and he or she may not even be aware of it. However, there is a situation during which the information exchange, spoken and unspoken, is so intensely concentrated that the communication land mines are very obvious to Mr. Whizbang. They hit him or her like a mallet. This situation is the Job Fair. For the uninitiated, a Job Fair is an event, usually held at a hotel, during which many companies get to interview many candidates for the positions they have open. Typically each company has a room or a suite and candidates file in one after another for a very brief interview. Because of the opportunity to meet a large number of applicants in one day, a Job Fair is a good way for a company to staff a new department or hire up a number of salespeople for a new territory.

I have attended more than a few Job Fairs in my professional life. Fortunately I have been on the Whizbang side of the desk for these events. Job Fairs are excellent examples of the pressurized situation where the candidate's communication skills, verbal and non-verbal, are the only things between him and a second interview and maybe a job. The candidate is under pressure to be compelling instantly. The company representatives are under pressure to staff up quickly without making a bad hire.

As each candidate walks in the suite, opinions are being formed, calculations are being made. How are they dressed? Do they look sharp? What does their resume look like? Any typos? Is it easy to follow? The candidate sits down and a brief chat begins. The exchanges are usually very similar. Are they compelling? Engaging? Do I want this person on my team? Representing my company?

The chat ends one of two ways. Either with "We'll keep your resume on file." Or "We'll call you to set up a time for you to come see us for a formal interview." This is why I retain a strange fondness for my Job Fair experiences. Every time someone walked into the room it was an all-or-nothing situation for both of us. And because of that, I was always paying extremely close attention to the person sitting across from me. If an applicant happened to trip a communication land mine it was impossible for me to miss it and unfortunately, my list of land mines grew.

I'm hoping that by writing this book I can make it easy for you to use my unique vantage point to your professional advantage.

Super Words and Phrases of Immeasurable Power

Beyond my list of communication land mines, I have also been compiling a list of Super Words and Phrases of Immeasurable Power. Used correctly, these words and phrases will give you brief, temporary Communications Super Powers.

Some of these words and phrases are useful as anti-detonation devices for certain types of communication land mines. Some are just words and phrases I've picked up along the way that I have noticed produce excellent results in conversation, in e-mail messages, or whatever medium you choose.

I will sprinkle these words and the explanation of their powers throughout the pages of this text. I include them because I have incorporated every one of them in my own professional vocabulary and I encourage you to do the same because I have seen them work. They work in a conversation the way the "Turbo!" button works in a video game.

Let me make an analogy to describe the relationship between video games and interpersonal communication fireworks:

During the winter of 1970, my Dad flooded our back patio in New Jersey. Overnight our patio turned into an ice rink. This turned out to be the perfect accessory for the presents our parents bought us that Christmas. My brothers and I all got hockey skates, sticks, and pucks that year, and so started my enduring love affair with the game of hockey.

Before long I was recruited by a local team of like minded five-, six-, and seven-year olds and their parents. Soon I was traveling all over New Jersey, Connecticut, and Pennsylvania playing hockey every weekend. This went on for years.

Typically my dad drove me to the games. During those trips when my Dad couldn't drive me I'd travel with the coach. This actually had a silver lining because my Dad would always hit me with $5 to buy a hot dog and a soda after the game.

I do not believe I ever bought a hot dog, a soda, or anything at all to eat. After each game I would quickly change the $5.00 into quarters. And thus I established the other pillar in my life, pinball. For many of my younger years, my entire universe revolved around pinball games and hockey pucks.

As I got older, video games took over and pushed the pinball machines into the back of the arcade. Undeterred, I would wade through the rows and rows of video games to find a pinball machine. This passion lasted through my college years. In a place called Campus Pizza there stood a pinball machine called "High Speed" which I beat on for four straight years. I think I was always attracted to pinball because the game itself is more physical than video games. To this day I'm still mostly a pinball guy.

But I do not resent the video games. I dabble in them now and again. But strangely I only like the driving games. Race cars, snowmobiles, motorcycles, I only like the race games. I'm a huge fan of Hot Pursuit, Virtua Racer, and that one where you get to race around the grounds of Alcatraz.

It is very common among the racing games that, through a certain combination of death defying feats, luck, and various Jedi mind tricks one can light the almighty Power Boost! button, Turbo! button, Nitrous! button, Lightspeed! button, or Whatever! button on the game's console.

As any good gamer knows, when it lights you just pound that thing and "kaboom!" your vehicle rockets forward with heart-stopping acceleration as you blow past everyone else on the track (or street, river, swamp, bog, fen, forest, system of underground tunnels, snowy landscape, deep space, post-nuclear conflict scorched earth, or whatever venue upon which you happen to be racing).

Using Super Words and Phrases of Immeasurable Power will light that button on your "communication console." The right words, whether spoken or written, can "light up" your business conversations, giving them the power and substance they need to communicate your desires, goals, and understandings effectively. The right words help you move from talking to Mr. Whizbang into *communicating* with him or her.

Throughout this book I will explain the powers and propose the potential usage of the following Super Words and Phrases of Immeasurable Power:

◆ Am I catching you at a bad time?
◆ I'll be brief.
◆ Advice.
◆ You don't have to chase me.
◆ Tight fit.
◆ Curious.
◆ What is the best possible outcome of this meeting?
◆ The Name of Mr. Whizbang's Company vs. "You Guys."

There are Four Communication Methods

In any given business situation, you can choose from these four communication methods:

◆ The phone
◆ E-mail
◆ Regular mail
◆ Face to face

Telepathy, Morse Code, smoke signals, messages in bottles, and interpretative dance aside, I submit the above as the definitive list of communication options open to every business person.

This book has four sections to mirror the four communication methods; however, it is not necessarily designed for the sections and chapters to be read sequentially. You can begin anywhere. You can start at the beginning and read through to the end, or you can check the table of contents and zero in on the land mine of your choice.

To be sure, land mines are everywhere in each category. However, once you've got them identified they become relatively easy to avoid. In fact, my experience has been that once I made a conscious effort to catalogue these land mines I began noticing the instances when my peers, my staff, and my superiors set them off. I expect your experience will be the same.

You may be as alarmed as I continue to be at how often business people are going about their day without the slightest regard for what impression their communication skills are having on the various audiences in their business lives. It is clear to me that business people for the most part are paying tremendous attention to their wardrobe, weight, hair, and cars, and paying little mind to their communication skills. But not you. No, no, no. You hold in your hands the land mine roadmap. And together we are going to set you apart from most other people in a very powerful way.

No matter whom you address – your subordinates, peers, superiors, or Mr. Whizbang – effective and compelling communication skills are your chief differentiators. However, given that there are four communication methods, keep this in mind: how *you* prefer to communicate is irrelevant. How *Mr. Whizbang* prefers to communicate is absolutely essential. If you are not getting a response from a particular Whizbang, my advice is to switch gears and try a different method. Maybe Mr. Whizbang's an e-mail person and you've been leaving voice mail messages. Maybe he or she would respond better to a letter rather than to an e-mail message. The point is you've got to find out which method goes with which Whizbang.

One of my clients is an excellent video production company we'll call MovieCo. One of their largest prospects was a rather large bank headquartered 60 miles away. They asked me to find that bank's Whizbang and open up a dialogue with him or her regarding the outsourcing of all their video work to MovieCo.

To give you an idea of scale, if MovieCo were to become the exclusive video production company for this bank they would increase their annual revenues by just over 30%. So I did my homework and found Mr. Whizbang, whose name for the purposes of this story is Janet. Janet was, and probably still is, the Vice President of Video Services. She was Mr. Whizbang.

Over the course of the next two weeks I called three times and sent a letter of introduction. No response of any kind came from their end. So I called again one morning and got her Administrative Assistant, Flora, and said "Hi Flora, it's Marty Clarke, catching you at a bad time? No? Ok, I'm trying to send Janet an e-mail message, can you tell me what her e-mail address is so I get it right?"

I sent a very quick e-mail message and Whammo! I got a response back from Janet. She couldn't meet with me but she wanted me to hook up with her second in command Jason. Jason was relatively easy to get on the phone and sure enough he had a project upon which he'd like us to bid.

We jumped on the opportunity and put our best foot forward with a well thought out proposal. In the end, MovieCo got the project and still produces a large amount of the bank's videos. While MovieCo's day-to-day contact is still Jason, Janet remains in the loop by e-mail and the occasional conference call.

The reason this story is so important from a communications standpoint is MovieCo never would have gotten that customer without getting to Janet through Jason. And we'd have never gotten there if I had not discovered through a little trial and error that Janet was an e-mail person. If I'd have kept calling her, we'd probably still be on the outside looking in.

Given the premise that there are only four ways to communicate (using the phone, e-mail, through regular mail, and in person) it should not be an arduous task to find out which method Mr. Whizbang prefers. Once you solve that mystery, the task is to avoid the land mines that exist within that medium. And as you will see, land mines are hidden in every communications method. The key is to spot them. If you can spot them you can get around them and by doing so, possibly set yourself apart.

Section One: The Phone

Repeat after me: "The Phone is the most dangerous thing on my desk."

Go ahead, say it. Here, I'll save you the trouble: The Phone is the most dangerous thing on your desk. This is the absolute truth. I wouldn't waste your time with conjecture.

I'm sure you can remember at least one painful encounter with an item on your desk at some point in your career. You may have poked yourself with your stapler, your pencil, or that thing that takes staples out of things. Even your Lucite "Rookie of the Month" award in the shape of a star could probably cause you grievous injury if you gave the project a little effort. But nothing, *nothing* on your desk is more dangerous than that phone.

> *Every time you pick up that phone and dial, picture yourself standing in a parking lot, knee-deep in a lake of gasoline with a lit road flare in your hand. Proceed with caution.*
>
> --M. Clarke

You must respect that every conversation is going to leave an impression on Mr. Whizbang, especially the first phone call.

Mr. Whizbang can hear that 100 Watt smile of yours on the phone. He or she can also tell when you are slouched in your chair, bored, and not entirely paying attention.

A phone call that goes bad can be a disastrous event. The impression of you that gets formed in Mr. Whizbang's mind is a fragile thing: stepping on a communications land mine on the phone can cause that impression serious damage. If you wind up having more than one conversation with Mr. Whizbang before you meet him or her, each conversation is going to contribute to that impression.

Consider this: a very common phenomenon in the business world is the case where two people may have numerous conversations with one another over the course of months, maybe even years, but they never meet. Sometimes events conspire and they finally wind up in the same place and meet one another. It is always a revelation when they each "put a face to the voice." And while it is true that relationships do form over time on the phone, *impressions* are made immediately. That is why the phone is the most dangerous thing on your desk. Unfortunately, it has been my experience that most people will prepare quite a bit more for a face-to-face meeting than they will for a phone call, and this is why the land mines that exist for that communication method are probably some of the most deadly.

CHAPTER 1: Land Mine!

Lack of Preparation

When I first started out in sales I was annoyingly eager. Oh, it's true! I look back on those days with equal amounts of amusement and abject mortification. But I had high energy, a positive attitude, and a blinding belief in the kindness of strangers--which are actually not awful traits for a beginner rep.

I remember well the day my first sales manager, Victor, called me into his office and handed me a thick file folder with the name EverQuik written on it in green marker. After only a few months on the job I was charged to succeed where so many in the office had failed. I was to crack the EverQuik account and bring it home. I went mental. Here was my chance to prove myself. This account was worth about six months of quota. Glory would be mine if I were able to attend the President's Club trip in my very first year in sales.

Within twenty-five minutes of that meeting I had discovered the name of EverQuik's President. His name was, and probably still is, Burt Bannerman. I told myself, "Must set an appointment with Burt. Start at the top." Soon, I convinced myself, I would be in Cancun, or Hawaii, or Boca Raton with all the other wildly successful sales reps.

Within about twenty-*six* minutes of my meeting with Victor I was at my desk and on the phone to EverQuik. For the next three weeks I tried unsuccessfully to get Burt Bannerman on the phone. Not once did I ever get him. I left messages. Sent letters. Not a peep out of the company's president. I tried catching him after hours. Tried getting him early in the morning. During lunch. Despite all my efforts I had come up empty.

If you've ever worked on a sales floor you've probably had the experience of working in cubicles. And no one knows more about your sales life than the people with cubes within earshot of yours. Tell your sales manager what he or she wants to hear; your cube mates know the real deal.

Early one morning Andy, the guy in the cube next to mine, leaned back so only his head stuck beyond the partition.

Andy: Hey Mart, you gonna call Burt again this morning?

Marty: Yep.

Andy: You think you'll get him?

Marty: Maybe. I figure he might be in early today.

Andy: What are you going to say to him if he picks up?

I would give a sizable amount of money to have a picture of my face after he said that. I was positively dumbfounded. Dumb struck. Dumb in general.

I never spoke to Burt that morning. And that was probably a good thing, because I wouldn't have had anything to say to the man if I had. He doesn't know it, but by being impossible to get on the phone, Burt saved me from stepping on a very embarrassing land mine. I was totally unprepared for the call. If I had gotten through to him it would have been my undoing. I would have stepped directly on the Lack of Preparation land mine in a very ugly way.

Lack of Preparation has always been a bad career move. In these days when information is a click away, there's just no excuse for stepping on the Lack of Preparation land mine. And yet, ill-preparedness is extremely common. Poor preparation becomes very obvious to the person on the other end of the phone. When I was on the Whizbang side of the desk I could usually tell when someone had not done any homework before calling me. They usually spoke about themselves exclusively and had little or no questions that were specific enough to signal that they knew something about me or my company.

Picture two calls to Mr. Whizbang:

"Hi Mr. Whizbang, my name is Marty Clarke, I'm with Product Inc. We've had great success in helping companies like yours reduce their whatever costs while at the same time improving their bottom line...."

Mr. Whizbang is now thinking of how to end this conversation. Isn't that sad?

Or,

"Hi Mr. Whizbang, my name is Marty Clarke. Am I catching you at a bad time? No? Ok, well I spent some time on your Web site yesterday and I definitely noticed a few places my company, Product Inc, could have a positive impact. I have a few quick questions about Whizbang Inc. that I was hoping you could answer for me....

The difference is monumental. The immediate impact on the call is that Mr. Whizbang is *engaged.* He or she can tell that this is no random cold call. While it may indeed be one of twenty-five calls a rep makes that day, it does not sound like it. The impact of good preparation is it gives you the ability to set yourself apart from the crowd of people who *are* just pounding out thoughtless cold calls.

Avoiding the Lack of Preparation Land Mine

A little homework goes a long way. You don't have to kill yourself doing it. Start with the company Web site. Pick any prospect you like and read their Web site and write down at least THREE questions that pop up in your head. Sounds simple and it is. But the difference will be noticed on the other end of the phone.

Keep in mind that every question should have something to do with why your company should be Whizbang's newest vendor/partner/strategic alliance. You may be curious why Mr. Whizbang chose to locate his company in Butner, NC, but that probably has nothing to do with what products your company provides, and that question is therefore moved to the "Stupid Question" bucket.

I've been to tons of training classes and motivational seminars and in each one I was assured "there are no stupid questions." I'm here to tell you that this is one of the biggest lies ever. There are plenty of stupid questions. With a little homework, you should be able to identify and avoid asking them.

Visit a prospective client's Web site as soon as possible. As you page through a Web site, make sure you pay attention to a few key areas:

The Management Team – Many companies post brief bios of each member of the management team. Read these. Read them all. Not only will they give you a roadmap to who's who in the organization, they also usually reveal something interesting about the company's culture. This may give you insights you can use in a conversation with Mr. Whizbang. For example, while I was doing research on a company I had the happy coincidence of finding that the CFO of a company I was targeting went to the same college I did. That appointment was relatively easy to set.

The Mission Statement – Do you think Mr. Whizbang had a hand in writing this or what? Even if he or she didn't, he or she approved it before it got posted on the company Web site. Because a mission statement embodies the core beliefs, values, and goals of an organization, the chances are very high that Mr. Whizbang was intimately involved with the creation of the company's mission statement. How better to differentiate yourself than by referencing it when you get him or her on the phone. Again, it only makes sense to mention its relevance to the services or solutions your company provides.

The Press Releases – If the company upon which you are calling posts press releases on its Web site and you do not take the time to read a few of the more recent releases before calling Mr. Whizbang, then you are a chucklehead of an incalculable magnitude. Your chuckleheadedness cannot be measured with conventional mathematics. If someone were to ask you how big a chucklehead you are, just answer "isosceles triangle" and continue to go about ruining your career.

Read the Press Releases before you call. Do it. I cannot express how important this is. If you read the press releases you instantly have a topic that will engage Mr. Whizbang quickly. Here is an example that illustrates how easy it is to use press releases to make a good impression:

"Hi, Mr. Whizbang, this is Marty Clarke from Product Inc. Am I catching you at a bad time? No? Great, I'll be brief. I was on your Web site yesterday and I read the press release where you announce Whizbang Inc. will be launching a new product set during the second quarter..."

Press releases are the easiest way to get a company's pulse, to find out what's going on. There are very few press releases published in the business world that have not passed through the editing hands of some of the highest ranking individuals of an organization.

All this assumes that you have some cyberspace experience and can use the various search engines and research tools available on the Internet these days. If you cannot, my advice is you need to acquire these skills immediately because they are essential. That said, following the three-question rule to prepare for a phone call and avoid the Lack of Preparation landmine is still the best indicator of how that first call will go. If after reading a company's Web site (or even doing your research in the public library) you cannot come up with three questions relevant to what your company provides, I would advise you *not* to pick up the phone.

One of my favorite things to do when I was a Big Shot Executive was to ask a potential vendor, "Hey Lenny, what did you think of our Web site?" That one was always good for separating the keepers from the sweepers. Whenever I asked that question it was immediately obvious who had taken the time to learn about my company and who was just burning through their call list.

Through the course of my years as a Corporate Ladder Climber I was always flattered when I received a cold call from a recruiter. Flattered as I was, the calls themselves were usually very similar in nature and I never reacted to them by engaging the headhunter in too long of a conversation. Except one. Her name was Julie. When Julie called me, she had me in her spell in two quick sentences.

Julie: Hi, this is Julie. Is this Marty Clarke?

Marty: Yes.

Julie: Well Marty, I've been reading about you and I had a question or two for you. Do you have a minute?

Reading? About me? Questions? Well, my stars, I had all the minutes she wanted.

Julie had called soon after I had been promoted to a certain level, and based on company policy, a press release had been sent to announce my promotion. Julie read my press release and turned it into a way to get my attention. Julie and I had a nice chat and I wound up giving her a lead on someone I knew who was looking for the kind of opportunity she was describing. But that's not the point. The point is that her call was entirely different than the other cold calls simply because Julie had prepared for the call by doing a little homework and engaged me with it immediately.

Worth Repeating

❖ Poor preparation becomes very obvious to the person on the other end of the phone.

❖ A little homework goes a long way.

❖ Pick any prospect you like, read their Web site and write down at least THREE questions that pop up in your head.

❖ Be sure you make your questions relevant to the products and services you provide.

❖ Read the bios of the Management team.

❖ Read the mission statement.

❖ Read the press releases.

CHAPTER 2: Land Mine!

The Instant Launch

The Instant Launch land mine gets triggered any time you get Mr. Whizbang on the phone and you immediately start talking and talking, never giving Mr. Whizbang a chance to participate in the conversation until you run out of breath.

This land mine used to make me crazy. I'd be at my desk, in the middle of something, and my phone would warble at me. I would pick up the phone and identify myself. Then I would be deafened by the sound of the Instant Launch land mine going off because I wouldn't be in the conversation for about another 120 seconds while the person on the other end told me all about what their company does.

And all that time, while that person is talking, inside my head I'm dying. I'm regretting ever having picked up the phone at all. Should have just let it go to voice mail, but nooooo, I had to pick it up. Stupid. Now I have Rep-Zilla reading me The Oxford English Dictionary. I have things I have to get done here. Drowning, I'm drowning in anxiety. If this kid doesn't take a breath soon I'm going to run screaming from the building, call the President of the United States and volunteer for an embassy position someplace far away.

Oh, I'm overreacting? I do not believe I am. Let me tell you, business people from every stratum in the organizational chart feel the same way. What? They are just sitting there waiting for the phone to ring and have a rep blather on and on? Nope. Thanks for playing. Good night. And please, drive home safely.

No one likes to listen to a motor mouth whose words keep falling out like an endless string of dominos. They talk, they talk, they talk, they say nothing. Do not be this person. Tripping the Instant Launch land mine will peg you as an unattractive cold caller immediately.

I have a theory that the Instant Launch is a knee-jerk reaction born out of fear. Keep talking. If you're talking you are controlling the conversation. The other person can't say "no" if you just keep going. I don't think any rep does this consciously. It's a rookie mistake. However, it's a mistake that isn't being made solely by rookies.

Another theory is that the Instant Launch is the result of laziness rearing its ugly head. Many times the caller is thinking: "I have my pitch. I have to make my X number of calls today and so here we go. If you give me an appointment, fine. As I'm saying my pitch I'm actually thinking about something else because I'm bored. I've memorized this pitch and have repeated it so many times that I'm sick of it myself."

When that mentality creeps in, it is usually because laziness allowed the mentality the opportunity to present itself. It may be a difficult task to keep your enthusiasm high but it's essential: if you do not, your lethargy will come through loud and clear on the phone.

Avoiding the Instant Launch Land Mine

This one is easy to avoid. An exceptionally wise idea in avoiding this land mine is to involve the person on the other end of the phone as soon as possible. Mr. Whizbang is not in his or her comfort zone when receiving a lecture. Also, all the research on adult learning suggests that adults are most receptive to new information when the transmission of that information involves some interaction. So be mindful to allow Mr. Whizbang to participate in the conversation as soon as possible. You might want to ask Mr. Whizbang something like:

"I'm from Product Incorporated, are you familiar with us?"

At this point Mr. Whizbang knows it is a cold call. Some folks might tell you that it is a bad idea to alert Mr. Whizbang to this so early in the conversation but I would stand respectfully on the other side of the debate table from those folks. If Mr. Whizbang has any interest whatsoever, he or she will let you proceed. If Mr. Whizbang lets you proceed, then you should get to the point of your call quickly. If not, the conversation is apt to be blissfully short. A blissfully short cold call is better than a long, protracted conversation that ends up wasting a lot of your time.

Handling Objections

Sometimes, asking this question has a strange benefit. This question has a habit of causing a reaction in Mr. Whizbang where his or her immediate response is an objection. For instance I've heard the following answers to this question:

"Yeah, read about you guys in the paper. You're the ones going bankrupt."

"Yes I am. You guys nearly put me out of business about two years ago."

"Yeah, but we don't need any Products right now."

"No, I don't, but lemme ask ya, you guys sell sheet rock? We had a wall collapse in the storm and there's nothing between us and the bagel place next door. You guys sell sheet rock? Install sheet rock?"

"Yes, I know about your company. About four of your competition called me today too."

When you ask the "Are you familiar" question and Mr. Whizbang shoots back with an objection or issue of any kind, as in these instances, you are in a position to make a split-second decision. Your decision must obviously be based in its entirety on what Mr. Whizbang's objection or issue is. In any event, you either decide to end the conversation quickly and respectfully so you can go on to a more productive phone call with someone else, or you address the objection directly.

There are many excellent texts that devote themselves to the art of handling objections. For my part, I'll say only this: if you ask the "Are you familiar" question and get hit with an objection, then whatever agenda you had going into this call has gone out the window. If you hear an objection early in the call and you decide to proceed, the best course of action is to wade right in. It is a fool's game to brush the objection aside and try to steer the conversation to your own agenda. The only point at which Mr. Whizbang will allow the conversation to proceed will be when his or her feelings about the objection have subsided. If Mr. Whizbang is objecting, at least he or she is paying attention. This is an opportunity to engage Mr. Whizbang.

DEFINITION
engage (verb): a) to hold the attention of, engross; b) to induce to participate

---

Being Ready to Continue

If Mr. Whizbang's answer to the "Are you familiar" question is "No, I am not. What does your company do?" you are on! Again, it is wise to get to the point as soon as possible. But clearly, the most important thing about this exchange is that you must be very ready with an answer that contains two elements:

1. *A quick, intelligent, and compelling answer to the question*

The emphasis here is on the "quick" part. I have heard many speakers, and read many books, that talk about the importance of having your "30-second commercial" ready at all times. A 30-second commercial may be handy and appropriate at a cocktail party, a Chamber of Commerce mixer, or in an initial appointment with a prospect, but on the phone I advise you to have a much shorter version of this saga on the tip of your tongue. Be advised, if you complete your 30-second commercial while on the phone with Mr. Whizbang, you have just jumped on the Instant Launch land mine.

Reducing your company's offerings and abilities down to a sentence or two is anathema to most sales reps and will ignite anxiety attacks in most marketing people. I feel the same way. Recognize this hesitation when it hits. It is natural not to want to do it. In fact, the prouder you are of what you and your company have to offer, the harder it is to boil those offerings and capabilities to their most elemental description. Do it anyway. Mr. Whizbang will appreciate your brevity and it will move the conversation along.

2. *What your company and this call have to do with Mr. Whizbang specifically*

After you've tossed out a tight sketch of what you or your company offers, you must then attach those concepts to Mr. Whizbang in particular. This connection has to be articulated in your head *before* you pick up the phone. Trying to articulate this connection in the moment, on the fly, often results in awkward and inefficient communication.

Take a minute to think of this before you dial. Write it down if you have to. The point is to tie your offering to Mr. Whizbang as an individual. Remember, the fundamental and inescapable question in Mr. Whizbang's mind every time you get him or her on the phone is not "Why are you calling?" it is "Why are you calling *me*?" Those who can communicate that connection quickly and clearly are going to be the ones who get to press on with the possibility to explore an opportunity.

Avoiding the Instant Launch land mine involves engaging Mr. Whizbang very early in the call, and the only way to do this is to ask him or her a question. If you've done your homework, questions should come easily to you. The key is to get one question, possibly your best one, out as early as you can in an effort to involve Mr. Whizbang.

Worth Repeating

❖ No one likes a motor mouth whose words keep falling out like an endless string of dominos.

❖ Allow Mr. Whizbang to participate in the conversation as soon as possible.

❖ If you hear an objection early in the call and you decide to proceed with it, the best course of action is to wade right in and address it.

❖ If you complete your "30-second commercial" on the phone with Mr. Whizbang, you have just jumped on the Instant Launch land mine.

❖ After you've tossed out a tight sketch of what you or your company offers, you must then attach those concepts to Mr. Whizbang in particular. This connection has to be articulated in your head *before* you pick up the phone.

Super Words and Phrases of Immeasurable Power

"Am I Catching You at a Bad Time?"

Aaaahhhh, the peace and serenity… Armed with this, you are fearless on the phone. If this phrase were removed from my everyday speech I would not know how to start a phone call.

Burn this question onto your mental C Drive and use it every time you pick up the phone. I use this phrase at the beginning of every call I make. I use it even when I call my Dad and he has to take my call.

This question should be the first thing out of your mouth after you introduce yourself. There are three typical responses to this phrase and I will list them for you here:

Marty: Am I catching you at a bad time?

Mr. Whizbang: Well Marty, there's never a good time, but I have a minute…

Be advised, there is a chance your prospect is being funny. Act accordingly. Do not herniate yourself laughing but play along. Offer to call back when it's more convenient and when Mr. Whizbang says "No, go ahead" you're on. It's a good idea at this point to preface your pitch by making some comment on how brief you are going to be:

"Ok, thanks, Mr. Whizbang. I promise not to tie you up here. I was on your Web site yesterday and …"

You will find Mr. Whizbang a bit more relaxed and ready to chat if he or she knows you are going to respect his or her time. This quick exchange will also build an immediate rapport.

Marty: Am I catching you at a bad time?

Mr. Whizbang: No, this is fine. What can I do for you?

Be advised, you're on. Get to the point. Be compelling and drive tactfully for the appointment. Do not under any circumstances make the prospect pay a price for giving you a shot by being long-winded. If you think by the inch but talk by the yard, you'll blow your opportunity by a mile. Refrain from littering the conversation with any nonessentials.

Marty: Am I catching you at a bad time?

Mr. Whizbang: Actually, Marty, I have three people in my office right now and I thought you were our CFO calling.

Be advised, you are standing on a land mine but it has not gone off. Do not jump up and down on it by going into your pitch. Apologize and get off the phone as politely as possible without sounding like a whimpering sycophant. When you do call back later, the prospect will be a bit warmer to you and regard you as someone who is respectful of his or her time.

Cultivating business relationships is an inexact science. There is no foolproof formula for creating an attractive image of yourself in someone else's mind. Creating engaging and productive conversations is a demanding task, especially on the phone. But you can safeguard your efforts by making sure your phone call is not an immediate inconvenience by using the phrase "Am I catching you at a bad time?" It sounds so simple but I encourage you to try it. You may find it might save you from damaging yourself before you even get started.

CHAPTER 3: Land Mine!

Wrath of the Rep

One of the laws of business is:"Not everyone calls everyone back."

This law is in action every day across America and probably all over the globe. It is *especially* prevalent, however, in the sales world. When I was an Exec, I admit I did not call every vendor back who cold called me and left a message. *Mea culpa.*

Back when I was a rep it bothered me when someone I cold called didn't call me back. Over time I came to expect it; however, it still bugged me. It probably bugs you. And from me to you, it's natural to feel this way. Feeling a tad piqued at the situation is acceptable. What's NOT acceptable is letting your prospect feel your furious wrath the minute you get him or her on the phone.

"Gee Mart, thanks for the sage advice but typically I don't show my prospects my 'furious wrath.'"

Oh, don't you? Yes or no, have any of the following sentences ever come out of your mouth when someone with whom you have been trying to get on the phone actually picks up?

"Mr. Whizbang. Hi, this is Marty Clarke. Boy, you sure are a hard man to catch up with." or "Hi Mr. Whizbang, this is Marty Clarke. You sure are a busy man." or (and this one's my favorite) "Mr. Whizbang. Hi, this is Marty Clarke over at Product Inc. It's great to *finally* get in touch with you."

Bang! Bang! Bang! Land mines are going off all over the place.

This is your wrath, your righteous indignation bubbling up and shooting right out of your mouth. Unfortunately the only thing you accomplish is putting your prospect on the defensive. Whenever a rep did this to me it would just irritate me no end.

Each one of those sentences is a particularly damaging land mine and so are the many variations on the theme. What you are really saying, no matter how nicely you say it, is:

"Hi Mr. Whizbang. I have tried to get you on the phone for two weeks now and you haven't called me back. But now that I have you on the phone, I'm going to vent my frustration on you, and then we can get down to business."

My point is that business people tend to be passionate, especially the ones who really believe in their products. The urge to indulge this anger may never subside. This is a land mine that you may have to battle for the rest of your life. But that is fine because you will avoid this land mine and let all the others out there go on triggering it.

Avoiding the Wrath of the Rep Land Mine

Get over it. Easier said than done, but get over it. You *are* annoyed and you are in the right. That's actually the worst part of it. You *are* in the right and so you are going to feel the urge to let your prospect know it.

> *Anger is the wind that blows out the candle of the mind.*
> --V, The Mafia Manager

I actually had a referral from a friend of mine who said, "I was talking with Mr. Whizbang over at Wrap-Around

Industries, and after I told him what your company did he said I should have you call him this afternoon."

So I called. I called for two weeks. This guy was either not actually as interested as my friend said he was, or he was bipolar. I sent him an e-mail message and it disappeared into a black hole.

I finally got him. Live. On the phone. And let me tell you it was all I could do not to smack him one for making me work so hard to get him. Oh baby, did I want to get a "Are *you* ever tough to get a hold of" off on him. But I didn't. This was not the time to trot out an angry parade of statements. Trust me, the impulse was there, but I suppressed my annoyance knowing that it would not only irritate Mr. Whizbang, but also hinder my ability to conduct a compelling conversation. He eventually gave me an appointment that led to a small but satisfactory contract.

DEFINITION

impulse (noun): a) a sudden spontaneous inclination or incitement to some usually unpremeditated action; b) a propensity or natural tendency usually other than rational

---

Another experience I had was with a Whizbang, who worked at a large insurance company. Mr. Whizbang told me on the phone "Oh Marty, actually this is a bad time, I'm about five minutes late for a meeting. But I read through your material and I do want to talk with you. Can I call you back after 3:00 today?" I told him this would be fine, I'd be at my desk for his call.

Not only did Mr. Whizbang not call back that day, he never called back. He broke his promise. My rage knew no limit. But business is business, and when I finally did catch up with him, I wanted to let him have it. But I resisted that impulse, pasted a smile on my face, and got down to business. This account never did go anywhere and does not rank highly as a sales experience.

Occasionally I feel that urge to this day. It never gets any easier not to indulge myself. I have to concentrate, and I would encourage you to do the same. Get used to noticing this feeling and make sure you jump over that land mine.

Now, it may happen that if you show a little character and avoid this land mine, your prospect may actually volunteer a spontaneous, "Oh, Marty, I have been so busy, I'm sorry I haven't called you back."

The proper response to this is "Not a problem." Nice job, you just stepped around a land mine and the call just got a little warmer in the process. Mr. Whizbang has acknowledged doing you a moderate disservice. That is a perfect opportunity to be magnanimous, show some professional maturity and make some real progress in building your relationship with Mr. Whizbang. He or she will appreciate it, I assure you.

Another reason why the phrase "no problem" or some variation on that theme is extremely valuable when Mr. Whizbang apologizes for not calling you back is that even though you haven't demanded any payback or gotten your pound of flesh, there is an unspoken understanding that Mr. Whizbang owes you one. This typically does not seal an entire deal but it can be an opportunity to gain an appointment or some key action that can move your efforts along.

Anger is one of the most powerful of human emotions. Even the most mature people I know have a tough time when their anger is ignited. Once anger starts, it is often very hard to get it to subside. A problem that compounds most people's issues with anger is that most times they just don't see it coming. That is why identifying the Wrath of the Rep land mine is so important. If you can *recognize* the professional situations that may lead you down an angry path, you are much more likely to be able to work around your impulsive reactions. Armed with this knowledge, you can turn an all-too common knee-jerk reaction into a mature, well-thought out relationship builder.

Worth Repeating

❖ Not everyone calls everyone back.
❖ It is NOT acceptable to let Mr. Whizbang feel your furious wrath the minute you get him or her on the phone.
❖ The only thing you accomplish is putting your prospect on the defensive.
❖ You are in the right. Get over it.
❖ If you can recognize the professional situations that may lead you down an angry path, you are much more likely to be able to work around your impulsive reactions.

Special Addendum: Voice Mail

Now *here's* a controversial subject: voice mail!
Let's get into it.

Love it or hate it, I don't think voice mail is going anywhere any time soon. Either deal with it well or avoid it at all costs.

Me, I choose to deal with it. I am certainly not above leaving someone a voice mail message. I think voice mail, used properly, is a very handy communication tool. Voice mail has merit in that it is a bit more personal than e-mail. It certainly can be a great way to leave quick instructions or reminders, or ask a quick question. So I am firmly pro voice mail. But I do know it is a medium fraught with some serious land mines.

One of the most prevalent perceptions people have about voice mail is its permanence. When you are leaving a voice mail message, you know intuitively that what you are about to say is being recorded. One and done. No second chances. The mechanical tone sounds and you are on.

> *I hope you know that this will go down on your permanent record.*
>
> --G. Gano

When you're faced with leaving voice mail, your message is being recorded and there is an inherent loss of control. My theory is that this tends to increase the pressure in the situation just enough for people to lose their wits a bit. And when that happens, the level of attention to detail just goes right out the window. It has been my experience that some folks start talking quicker than they usually do. They often lose their own train of thought. I had the experience more than once of a person leaving me a message, messing it up, and then calling back with clarifications and apologies.

When I was a sales rep I used to be thrilled when I got back to my desk, dialed into my voice mail inbox and discover I had many messages waiting for me. It's a good sign when a sales rep is getting a lot of calls.

Truth be told, when I first started out in Sales (just after the Earth cooled) there was no voice mail. Our company receptionist, Betsy, answered the phones at the front desk and recorded who called whom on little pink slips of paper. Ancient history I know, but it was pretty easy to whip through the stack, pick out the important ones and get going.

Centuries later when I became an Exec, voice mail had been invented and I developed a very different reaction to having my voice mail inbox jammed with messages. Sometimes when I'd get back to my office after attending some meeting of egregious length I would know that my voice mail inbox would be full. As I stepped into the elevator, pushed the button for my floor, I could smell it. My voice mail inbox would be brimming with message after message. Not only had this meeting wasted my entire morning but I was about to spend even more time wading through messages.

So instead of being psyched about it, this situation would give me great anxiety. And often my deepest fears would be confirmed when I dialed into my mailbox only to hear the nice woman's voice drop the big one on me:

"You have *twenty-two* new messages. To listen to your messages, press one. To incinerate your phone and run screaming from the building, press two......"

You know, she never actually gave me that second option, but if she did, I'd have hit that two button in a heartbeat. Why did I cringe at the sound of that woman telling me I had all those messages?

The answer is I knew I'd be trapped next to the phone with my notepad and pen. I'd be sitting there for ages listening to land mines going off left and right, and not even exciting land mines. Voice mail is the electronic home of bone-numbingly boring messages. Oh it would take forever to get through them all. The Voice Mail Death March. I truly hated it.

During my tenure as Mr. Whizbang, I flew in a few private aircrafts, had a primo parking space, and sat in every luxury box in every sports arena from Raleigh to Tampa. These were excellent perks, no doubt. But I am here to tell you, perks are great, however nothing, NOTHING comes close to having your own administrative assistant.

The single greatest thing my Administrative Assistant, Doris, did for me was to clear out my voice mail inbox and hand me summaries. Doris would walk the Voice Mail Death March for me. Awesome. Unfortunately, we were downsized and Human Resources "modified her responsibilities" and Doris was "reassigned to a new Department" which is HR talk for "Listen to your messages yourself, punk." Easy come, easy go.

In the final analysis, I would venture that voice mail tries the patience of most business people. The trick is not to avoid voice mail. The trick is to use it to set yourself apart by NOT setting off the land mines that are illustrated in the next few chapters.

I reiterate, just knowing what land mines are there may make it easier for you to avoid them. And as you begin to avoid them two things will happen for you:

◆ The pressure will evaporate. You'll be a bit more confident when the tone sounds because you'll be concise and compelling.

◆ You will also let Mr. Whizbang know that you are respectful of his or her time, and above all, professional.

CHAPTER 4: Land Mine!

The Endless Message

This is the land mine that has given voice mail a bad name. This is the one that makes Mr. Whizbang recoil in horror every time he or she hears your recorded voice on the other end of the phone. Fix this one, avoid this one land mine and you are going to set yourself apart from 51% of your peers. Minimum.

The Endless Message, while a familiar demon, may be one of the hardest land mines to avoid. Keep in mind, the Endless Voice Mail is sneaky. It's got the Romulan Cloaking Device. It's that invisible girl from The Fantastic Four. The Endless Message land mine creeps in like the fog and you don't notice it until you're completely trapped.

Giving you reasonable benefit of the doubt, I'm sure you do not mean to go on and on with an Endless Message. I don't think anyone decides "Hey, I know, I'll pick up the phone here and ramble on aimlessly until I figure out what I want to say. Then I'll hang up. Good plan."

No, I do not think that of you in the slightest.

The sneaky part of this land mine comes in when you are in the middle of leaving a message and because you are unprepared to do so, you search around for your point until you realize you've gone on way too long without one.

I've done it. I'm not proud of it but I've done it. And if you are like me, it is not a pleasant feeling to realize you're in the middle of leaving an Endless Message.

Also, on a personal note, I've always found the phrase "Sorry for the long voice mail" at the end of an Endless Voice Mail to be somewhat infuriating. It's like saying "Hey, I know I've been beating on you like a rented mule, draining your life force for the last 95 seconds, but I'm sorry. Here, let me spit on you - and dent your car, too, before I hang up." Possibly I'm a bit oversensitive, but I don't think so. You may not find it offensive, but I am irritated when people say that. It adds insult to injury.

The strange thing is that the Endless Message, while a rookie mistake, is certainly not isolated to rookies. I've had Endless Messages left for me by some of the most professional people I know. Every time I receive one I revise my opinion of the person who left it. The Endless Message says to the person on the other end "Hello, regardless of what initial impression I've made, right now I'm a black hole sucking time and energy out of your day."

I can forgive someone for tripping this land mine once. Once. It happens to everyone. Any one can take his or her eye off the ball. But if you make a habit of it, or worse, gain a reputation for it, this land mine can be the kiss of death. You'll walk around your office or your territory with a Scarlet "E" for "Endless" on you and you won't even know it unless some good natured, leadership minded soul points out to you that your messages are renowned for being tedious, pointless, and endless. This is a reputation you do not want. When crafting your professional image, this should be avoided.

Everything you do, say, wear, or write is going to have an impact on Mr. Whizbang's opinion of you. It is going to have an impact on that "personal brand." Triggering the Endless Message land mine is going to do great damage to that opinion.

Avoiding the Endless Message Land Mine

Look before you leap.

An ounce of prevention is worth a pound of cure.

Pick whatever aphorism you like, but know what your point is *before* you leave a message. This is harder than it seems. Before you pick up that phone, think about what your point is. Write it down if you like. I do it all the time. During my normal business day my head's going 100 miles an hour. If I feel there may be a better than average chance I might not get Mr. Whizbang live and get forced to leave a message, I avoid this land mine if I write down two or three words about my point.

The first time I did that I was embarrassed. Years ago I had a boss named Tex. Tex left me instructions to leave him a detailed message on the progress, or lack thereof, on a particularly important project. I knew he would probably pick this message up in an airport, in between planes. Tex was not a very patient man and even though he wanted a "detailed message" leaving him an Endless Message would have been extremely unwise. So there I was at my desk, ready to leave the message and I felt like such an obsessive loser, writing down the points I wanted to make so I wouldn't leave anything out, and not yammer on *ad nauseum*. The situation was made worse when my buddy, Goodman, popped his head over my cubical wall:

Goodman: Mart.

Marty:(Not looking up) What?

Goodman: What are you doing?

Marty: Nothing.

Goodman: You coming to lunch with us or what?

Marty: I'll catch up.

Goodman: What are you writing notes on?

Marty: Tex wants an update on the Maniago project.

Goodman: Tex is in Miami.

Marty: I have to leave him a message.

Goodman: (Smiling) So you're writing notes before you leave him a message?

Marty: (still not looking up) Yes.

Goodman: Loser.

Marty: I'll catch up.

Goodman: Looooooooooooser.

Marty: I will catch up with you guys in a minute.

Goodman: Dude, can I just tell you that you are not even invited anymore.

Marty: If you leave me alone I can get this done and I'll probably be there before you order.

Goodman: Ok, but you have to sit at a different table.

Marty: Fine. Now go.

Goodman: Mart.

Marty: (looking up) What?

Goodman: Loser.

That exchange did not make me feel any better. Half of me actually agreed with Goodman. But I pressed on, and once I had it all in front of me, I was able to leave a short message with all the information Tex needed.

I was embarrassed the *first* time I did that. However, it worked so well that ever since then I have made it a very common practice of mine to write a few quick notes down before I leave a message. Now it's part of how I work.

Keep your messages short and simple. Even if you are a spellbinding conversationalist, keep your messages concise and to the point. Voice mail is the place to communicate pertinent facts. Voice mail is *not* the place to tell the entire story. Here is an example:

When I was in marketing, my company hadn't yet made the giant leap into the age of electronic information. My department used to produce a ton of printed material for our sales force: brochures, one-pagers, leave-behinds, white papers, site sellers, order forms, you name it. We were a printer's dream account.

Unfortunately our sales rep from the printing company, who was in every other way an excellent sales professional, had a habit of telling the whole story every time he left a message:

"Hi Marty, this is Donny from 123 Printing? Yeah, um, we did find out what the delay on your um, the new product brochures you wanted. Um, they got delayed because, well the first thing was our guys didn't use the right color codes on the initial run so when we got a look at..."

At this point I am listening to the Endless Message land mine go off and descending deeper and deeper into shell-shock. "Get to the point! Get to the point!" I think to myself, "Please. I have an entire blank page ready for this. Please get to the point."

Even though I want to, I cannot just delete Donny's message. I have to listen to the entire thing because somewhere in Donny's feeble attempt to leave a coherent message he is going to tell me when my brochures are going to be ready. I need that information so I can get my boss, Spike, off my back. Just like Tex, Spike was a boss who did not like to wait for an answer.

Back to Donny. I think he's nearing the end:

"...looked great and your folks signed off on it so we should be good to go in about, ummmmm, they're telling me we should ship the new product stuff on looks like the 12th. Ok, well, like I said, um, we had a miscue here on our end and that sort of started the ball off on the wrong foot. So we should be ok for now, you should see, well, if we ship on the 12th you guys should get it like... um, well pretty much you should get the stuff on like maybe the 15th. Ok? Let me know if you have any questions. I'm out of the office tomorrow but I'll be in all of today."

Here's how that message should have gone:

"Hi Marty, this is Donny from 123 Printing. I have your new product brochures shipping on the 12th. They should be on your doorstep by the 15th. Sorry for the delay. I'll follow up with an e-mail. If you need me, my number is 123-4567. Or use my cell phone at 123-987-6543. Thanks."

Gee, I say to myself, that Donny is a right to the point kind of guy. What a pleasure.

Actually, leaving a concise, to-the-point voice mail message will rarely result in any kind of outwardly positive response from Mr. Whizbang. He or she probably won't even notice it. But you won't have done yourself any damage and that is enough to make the effort. Even though Mr. Whizbang will not throw you a parade just because you avoided a land mine, if you do make a habit out of being concise, your customers, prospects and colleagues, even if they don't realize it consciously, will appreciate it.

While it is important to be well thought out and prepared for any phone call, the need for compelling brevity is even more important when leaving a voice-mail message. Have a clear idea of what you are going to say before you pick up the phone. Write it down if you like. I do. You may feel a little silly the first time you do it like I did. But I am here to testify that this method works. When I write down a few notes before leaving a message, I find I am much more confident and this comes across in my voice as I speak. I hope you will try it. Whatever you do, do not drone on with the cosmetic details surrounding your point. If you do, you have removed the convenience factor from voice mail and stepped on a very destructive land mine.

Worth Repeating

❖ The sneaky part of this land mine comes in when you are in the middle of leaving a message and because you are unprepared to do so, you search around for your point until you realize you've gone on way too long without one.

❖ Everything you do, say, wear, or write is going to have an impact on Mr. Whizbang's opinion of you. It is going to have an impact on that "personal brand." Triggering the Endless Message land mine is going to do great damage to that opinion.

❖ Know what your point is *before* you leave a message.

❖ Keep your messages short and simple. Voice mail is not the place to tell the entire story.

❖ Write down a few notes before you leave a message that you know has the potential to be "Endless."

Super Words and Phrases of Immeasurable Power

"I'll Be Brief."

> *Brevity is the soul of wit.*
> W. Shakespeare

If ever you worked for me on my staff, you would have been introduced sooner or later to an apparently annoying habit of mine which is to dispute immediately the phrase "I did not have time." Whenever someone who reported to me told me that something I wanted them to get accomplished did not get accomplished because they "did not have enough time" I would immediately remind them that since everyone has the same amount of time per day, 24 hours, that could not be so. In fact it did not even make sense. I would alert them that, from my point of view they had the time but they must have used it on something else. Or, turning a pithier phrase, I would shoot back "Yes you did, you just didn't make the time for this."

I worked in a rather secure building and this was a very good thing because that prevented my staff from bringing in a Taser™ gun or possibly a bazooka to use upon me when I would do this to them.

I'll admit it. It is possible I am obsessed with time. But it was my tour of duty on the Whizbang side of the desk that made me so. All Whizbangs are obsessed with time. They all have more to do each day that can actually be accomplished each day. My number one fear, every time I answered my phone, was that the caller, as yet unknown to me, was going to waste my time. All Whizbangs have this fear. Consider this, why is it when you download something from the Internet, a file, a song, a picture, anything, many programs provide a window telling you exactly how much information has transmitted and how much more time the download is expected to last? Why, when the airplane has climbed to an acceptable altitude, does the pilot come on the intercom with "Hi folks, this is Captain Billy from the flight deck, looks like clear skies all the way to Boston today. Scheduled flight time this morning is one hour and fifty-one minutes...?" Why, pray tell, do the most popular rides at Disney World have giant signs out in front of them with messages that tell anyone within 100 feet how long, to the minute, the current wait time is for that particular attraction? The answer is simple: in any given situation, the question on everyone's mind is "How long is this going to take?" This question is born out of fear. That fear is articulated as "I hope this doesn't take too long." And the higher up you go in the business food chain the more severe that fear is.

The caller who allays this fear quickly will get a listen. And in my own professional life I am fond of using the phrase "I'll be brief" not only on the phone, but in e-mail and during face-to-face exchanges too. It never fails to produce an almost palpable reduction in the natural tension existing in any business situation.

That is why "I'll be brief" is on the list as a Phrase of Immeasurable Power. This phrase is a "Just Relax" grenade. Lob it in there early and Mr. Whizbang is all yours. Well, maybe that overstates the case. But it will go very far in reducing Mr. Whizbang's natural apprehensions.

Some folks twist this phrase around and do themselves huge damage in the process. Many were the rep or job seeker who got me on the phone and said:

Caller: Hi, Mr. Clarke?

Marty: Yes?

Caller: Hi, my name is Henry Richards. I got your name from Zelda down in IS? She said you have a position open for a trainer.

Marty: That's a fact. You a trainer?

Caller: Well, listen, I don't want to waste your time, but I was…

Waste my time? Nice self confidence there, Henry. Or is it that you are hopelessly coy, making the idea of smacking you on the top of your head with a crab mallet infinitely more attractive to me than offering you a job?

Either way, my opinion of Henry is plummeting.

Please take the phrase "I don't want to waste your time but…" and remove it from your professional vocabulary. After you do, take it to the back yard and burn it. Then bury the ashes out of state. Replace this phrase with "I'll be brief" and you will not only put Mr. Whizbang at ease you will also save yourself from the pitiless well of his or her poor opinion of you.

CHAPTER 5: Land Mine!

Phone Number at Mach Speed

Whenever I'm asked to speak publicly on the subject of business communication and the land mines that go along with it, I never fail to mention the "Phone Number at Mach Speed" land mine because it seems to be an extremely common trouble spot. Somewhere along the line, I'm sure everyone has heard somebody else rattle off their phone number in rapid-fire fashion.

Let's say Mr. Whizbang is listening to his or her voice mail and it's a message to which he or she definitely wants to reply. The caller leaves a perfectly fine message until he or she says, "If you want to call me back, it's wonetwseveneightnighnighfowunsevnighoh."

The phone number is indecipherable. Mr. Whizbang, pen in hand, was able to get maybe four of the necessary seven or ten numbers down. And if Mr. Whizbang does not know how to rewind the message, he or she is forced to go back and listen to the whole thing again.

And even if Mr. Whizbang *does* know how to rewind the message, why make this one stupid mistake and inconvenience him or her just because you decided to drop the hammer and say your entire phone number in the space of a second and a half?

At its worst, this land mine goes off at the end of an Endless Message. Whenever that happens to me my head just about spins off my neck. The pain inflicted by an Endless Message is enough, making the other person sit through it another time just to get your phone number is just plain cruel. What causes this? What causes reasonable people with usually gorgeous vocal cadence to morph suddenly into oral speed demons?

I'll tell you my theory. Most people do not *intentionally* rush through their phone number and sound like they've got a mouthful of pizza and lawn clippings. I do not believe this is intentional, but I do believe it is lazy.

One of the things you know without thinking is your phone number. That's the problem. You know it without thinking and so you say it without thinking. You just spit it out. Wham! And then you're on to other things. The phone number usually comes at the end of the message and so there's this mad-dash mentality that kicks in for some reason and you rush to finish your message. This is especially damaging because you want to leave Mr. Whizbang with the absolute *best* impression of your communication skills. Why step on this land mine and leave him or her with just the opposite?

Avoiding the Phone Number at Mach Speed Land Mine

I was born and spent the first 25 years of my life in Northern New Jersey. The good people of New Jersey tend to speak rapidly and I was no exception. And even though I retain little or no New Jersey accent, I still speak at a pretty fast clip. I will admit that as hard as I am on those who trip this land mine, I constantly have to remind myself not to rattle off my phone number. As a sales rep I'm sure I was a consistent offender. It was only when I moved onto the

Whizbang side of the desk that I got a good feel for how annoying this land mine can be. Speaking slowly on the phone does not come naturally to me, and so this is one of those land mines for which I must be on the constant outlook.

Here are a few ways to avoid this land mine:

The Take a Beat Method

Most phone numbers start with one or two sets of three numbers. Your area code, if you need to supply it, has three numbers, and your exchange also has three numbers. The trick is to wait a beat after you give out each set of three numbers. I do that even when I'm purposely slowing down a bit to make sure the person is going to get my numbers correctly. In other words, say "…my number is 123 (beat) 456 (beat) 7899." Using this method will interrupt the tendency to reel off an intelligible string of numbers.

The Two Times Method

Another good trick is to get into the habit of saying your telephone number twice in each message. You can say it at the beginning of your message, right after you say your name. And then you can repeat it at the end of your message. This is a great convenience to Mr. Whizbang who may not have gotten the entire number the first time you said it.

The Business Card Method

If you are in the habit of speaking rather quickly, a great way to avoid this land mine is to tape one of your business cards to your phone or your computer. When you are leaving Mr. Whizbang a message and it comes time to tell him or her your telephone number, read it off your business card. This will force you to slow down. The reason most people speed up their speech when they give their phone number is because they are doing it from memory. If you read it instead, you will block this natural tendency.

These methods sound rudimentary, and they are. However, even though this land mine is extremely easy to avoid, for some reason business men and business women are stepping on it all the time. The Phone Number at Mach Speed land mine probably has not caused anyone to lose a sale, miss out on a job, or fail to get into the college of his or her choice, but it is an irritant to the people who make the decisions on those efforts. So my advice is, if it is easy to get around this land mine, make the effort to do it and save Mr. Whizbang the trouble.

Worth Repeating

❖ Making the person sit through your message a second time in order to get your phone number is just plain cruel.

❖ The Phone Number at Mach Speed land mine is born out of laziness.

❖ Take a beat after saying your exchange and your area code.

❖ Say your number at the beginning of your message and at the end.

❖ Read your number off your business card.

CHAPTER 6: Land Mine!

Calling Every Day

If you leave a voice mail message for Mr. Whizbang every day for more than two days running, you are on your way to giving an extremely poor impression. I'm all for persistence, but there's a point where persistence becomes pushy. For example, whenever I'd have someone calling me every day it always struck me, "Am I this guy's only prospect or is he calling *everybody* every day?" Regardless, the prospect of getting together with this guy is not very attractive. He seems desperate.

I had a boss who actually forwarded a voice mail message to me with the instructions "Mart, find out what this guy wants. Do whatever you want but get him off my back." While my boss maybe should have done this himself, the experience taught me a lesson about what goes on in the mind of Mr. Whizbang when he or she notices that a caller keeps trying incessantly.

Desperation is an unattractive trait to be sure. Calling Mr. Whizbang once a day for an extended period of time will certainly send the message that you are desperate, even if you are not. Stepping on this land mine will create in the mind of Mr. Whizbang a few other messages, none of which I'm sure you want to send:

Bad Message #1: Mr. Whizbang is just another name on the call list

While this may or may not be true, the impression is almost unavoidable. If that message gets created in Mr. Whizbang's mind, the result is pretty bad: you've just marginalized Mr. Whizbang and his or her company by giving the impression that they are just names and numbers, and that they are not special in any way. It is tough to come back from that one. Everyone loves to be singled out and made to feel uniquely valued. No one likes to be lumped in with the crowd and treated like so much cattle. Once you make Mr. Whizbang feel like he or she is just one of the crowd, you have essentially said "There is nothing special about you." If that is the case it will be a very hard task to make him or her feel as if you are trying to get in touch because what you have to offer matters to them specifically.

Bad Message #2: You have a lot of time on your hands

People who call incessantly may actually be very busy people with a lot of clients, but it does not appear that way from the Whizbang perspective. It looks like all you do is sit on the phone and bang out cold calls. Everyone makes cold calls. Cold calls are the backbone of the economy. But repeated calls to Mr. Whizbang over a period of days looks like that is all you do. I assure you that if Mr. Whizbang gets the idea that you have a lot of time on your hands, he or she is not going to feel very compelled to spend some of his or her time with you.

Bad Message #3: You are an amateur

If you insist on Calling Every Day you are going to seem desperate. Pros, real business professionals, would never appear this desperate. Stepping on this land mine ought to be reserved for rookies looking for their first sale or trying to get their first job. If Mr. Whizbang were to describe you, which sentence would you prefer:

"She's a real pro." or "She's an amateur."

Clearly the latter is a huge negative. Being described as an amateur in almost any business arena is rarely a good thing. Mr. Whizbang does not want to deal with amateurs. He or she does not have the time, patience, or inclination to help you learn the ropes of your own trade. Even if you are trying to gain an entry level position of some sort and it is *expected* that your experience level will be low, casting yourself as having very professional communication skills can be a strong differentiator. It gives the hiring manager the impression that since you are, at least, an excellent communicator with the ability to conduct yourself professionally, there is something for them to build on as they groom you for bigger and better things.

Bad Message #4: You're a pest

On the very end of every business technology, every business solution, every sales pitch is a human being. If you bombard Mr. Whizbang with a phone call every day (or more), Mr. Whizbang is not going to be very interested in letting someone like you into his or her business life. The business day is demanding enough. Mr. Whizbang is naturally going to gravitate toward those people who make life easier for him or her. If the word "pest" ever pops up in Mr. Whizbang's mind in relation to his or her opinion of you, I'm afraid you may not be doing business with Mr. Whizbang ever, or much longer. Pests are time consuming. Pests are annoying.

I once managed a team of twenty-two people. I had a few managers who split the team members among them, but I was always very accessible to everyone on the staff.

Many were the times when someone would walk into my office with an issue and I would be able to judge immediately how time intensive the interaction was going to be just by who walked in. Some folks just naturally took up a ton of time. I loved them all and would never refer to them as "pests." Never. (Even though a few of them, on a few isolated occasions, may have been worthy of the description.) However, when these folks appeared at my door, I'd have to make a conscious effort to show no apprehension in my face or tone of voice even though I was genuinely concerned that my day was about to slip into a black hole.

Most team members took a reasonable amount of time. But there were a select few who possessed an excellent quality. Some folks on my team had the natural ability to be blissfully quick about resolving whatever they needed resolved.

One such team member was a woman to whom I'll refer as Meredith. What a pro. I only hope that you will have Merediths in your professional life. I was lucky enough to have her on my team. I think the reason Meredith and I got along so well was because we both knew she understood her job 1,000% better than I did and I was smart enough to stay out of her way and let her do it. On the few occasions when Meredith appeared in my office needing me to help her get something done or approved, I knew she would have whatever issue it was at the time pared down to:

◆ This is what's happening.
◆ This is what's wrong/needed.
◆ This is what I need you to do.

Quick. To the point. A model of efficiency. Whatever the polar opposite of "pest" is, that word would be the adequate description of Meredith. When she and those like her appeared at my door I became energized. I knew we were going to get down to business quickly. We were going to get something done.

Mr. Whizbang is a human being. He or she is going to have some sort of emotional response to you. If you step on the Calling Every Day land mine and beat him or her about the head and shoulders with repeated phone calls, that response is bound to grow negative and as such, Mr. Whizbang will shy away from you instead of engaging you.

Bad Message #5: You have no imagination

Although I will not explain the circumstances that surround why she told me this, my mother once told me that part of the clinical definition of insanity is "expecting different results to come from identical or similar causes." For example, let's suppose a person adds two plus two and gets four. That person works the same equation five straight times, getting four as the answer in each instance. An insane person might propose that when we add two plus two for the sixth time, we may get three.

I have no clue where my mother happened upon this information or even if it is true, owing to my mom is a librarian and not a psychiatrist. But that is not the point. The point is that by calling, unsuccessfully, each day you are telling Mr. Whizbang that you have no imagination. While Mr. Whizbang may not think you insane, certainly he or she will categorize you as "dense."

Take a different path. Try a new tack. Think of all the communication methods you have available to you. To continue to stick with just one method after having no results is eventually going to tell Mr. Whizbang that you are a bit slow on the uptake. This is not good, I assure you.

I discuss in the Preface of this book that determining what communication method your particular Mr. Whizbang prefers can be a good way to speed you along on your shot to impress him or her. Simply put, if all you do is call, you are telling Mr. Whizbang that you have no imagination at all or at least making the very minimal effort to make a connection with him or her.

Avoiding the Calling Every Day Land Mine

A call here, an e-mail message there, maybe a nice handwritten note - a little variety goes a long way. But that's the easy answer.

The deeper answer is that it has been my experience as a rep making calls, a sales manager with a team making calls, and as a marketing manager getting calls, that when this land mine crops up it is directly related to one of two things: either elephant hunting or lack of prospecting. Sometimes, it's both because one can actually lead to the other quite easily.

Elephant Hunting

The elephant is the universal symbol of largeness. True, there are plenty of things bigger than an elephant. Mountains, high schools, and ocean liners can all be counted upon to be larger than an elephant. But when something is described as being "big as an elephant" we intuitively know that the thing being described is inordinately large.

In business, elephant hunting is a phenomenon that occurs when a job applicant, a sales person, or anyone gets hyper-focused on the benefits of bagging the big one. The big job, the big account, the big donation, whatever you have occupying the center of your radar to the exclusion of anything else -- that's the elephant. Once somebody gets an elephant in their sights they tend to focus on it every day.

They stop paying attention to the basics and land mines start going off.

This land mine reminds me of a terrible story of a sales person I knew. We'll call him Eric. In 1992, Eric was trying to crack the Dryden Foods account. If he sold this account he would have been the king of the sales floor. However, he eventually rode that account right out the door. In his efforts to sell Dryden Foods he neglected all his other accounts and prospects so much that he got to be a joke around the office. Once he got the Dryden Foods account in his sights, he got tunnel vision and lost sight of everything else. A few months later our manager told him he either had to close the account that month or make his quota some other way or he was gone. He didn't make it.

While he was working the account Eric jumped up and down on the Calling Every Day land mine. He called the same people at Dryden daily for weeks. I never found out what they thought of him, but after a while I'm sure they got tired of him. He truly became a desperate man and his actions showed it.

Lack of Prospecting

Because he was so focused on one account, Eric never kept up with the necessary activities that would give him sales opportunities with multiple companies. A rep with very few prospects will tend to step on the Calling Every Day land mine if they are not careful. Once despair sets in, the person either prospects very hard and fills up his or her funnel with opportunities, or focuses even harder on the few prospects they do have. I call this kind of response "emotional mathematics." It usually involves a person spending more attention on fewer and fewer prospects. Simple math tells us this can lead easily to desperation and soon the Calling Every Day land mine has been triggered.

Unfortunately I've seen this happen to more than just Eric. Down in Florida, I saw a rep named Joe spend an entire summer trying to sell the Don Puzio resort. That account sank him. Donny Murdoch out in Boca Raton tried to sell the Team Windex account for seven months. He never got it and he never recovered.

You might think you're immune to this land mine and I hope you are, but keep an eye out just in case. Keep a very close eye on the frequency with which you call Mr. Whizbang. Be sensitive to the fact that even if you have not spoken to him or her, just the fact that you continue to call is building an impression of you in his or her mind. If you are getting no response, make sure you vary your approach. This will not only save you from appearing desperate, it may cause Mr. Whizbang to respond if you hit upon his or her preferred method of communication.

Worth Repeating

❖ If you leave a voice mail message for Mr. Whizbang every day for more than two days, you are on your way to giving an extremely poor impression.

❖ Desperation is an unattractive trait to be sure.

❖ Once you make Mr. Whizbang feel like he or she is just one of the crowd, you have essentially said "There is nothing special about you."

❖ If Mr. Whizbang gets the idea that you have a lot of time on your hands, he or she is not going to feel very compelled to spend time with you.

❖ Being described as "an amateur" in almost any business arena is never a good thing.

❖ On the very end of every business technology, every business solution, every sales pitch is a human being.

❖ Once somebody gets an elephant in their sights they tend to focus on it every day. They stop paying attention to the basics and land mines start going off.

❖ Even if you have not spoken to him or her, just the fact that you continue to call is building an impression of you in his or her mind.

❖ To continue to stick with just one method after having no results is going eventually going to tell Mr. Whizbang that you are a bit slow on the uptake.

Super Words and Phrases of Immeasurable Power

"Advice"

Never ask for information. Ask for advice.

Information is cold, impersonal, and everyone is asking for it. Advice, on the other hand, is warm, very personal, and no one is asking for it. Except me. And now you. Asking for advice when you want information is a great way to get Mr. Whizbang talking.

Let's look at two business interactions. Both ask a question trying to get the same data.Here's interaction number 1:

"Mr. Whizbang, can you share some information about Whizbang Inc with me?"

How mundane. How pedestrian. How positively "land mine-ish." Mr. Whizbang has heard this one a few times. Possibly a few times today alone. Mr. Whizbang is probably thinking you must be another sales rep, or somebody looking for a job. He or she will view it as another annoying solicitation. Bah!

Asking for information in this manner will bore Mr. Whizbang to tears. Soon he or she will pawn you off on someone else. Why? Mr. Whizbang has no time for this. He or she did not get up today to make sure you had enough information. It is as simple as that.

Information is not one of my favorite words. It has no super powers. Carefully chosen words will hold business conversations together.

> *Communication is not just words...It is the interaction of human beings sharing experiences and imparting ideas.*
> --William Marsteller, advertising exec

Let's move on to interaction number 2.

"I'm doing some research on Whizbang Inc. and I was hoping you could give me a little advice."

Wham! Mr. Whizbang is 150% more inclined to talk with you. The request is warmer and more personal. Also, I suspect very few people have asked Mr. Whizbang for her advice today. When you ask people for information, they tend to clam up or start to drift on you. The reason for this is because *everyone* is asking for information. All day, every day business people are either asked to give information or asked to digest information. The common phrase for this is "information overload." The Police released a song on their *Ghosts in the Machine* album called "Too Much Information" and that was over *two decades ago*. The key here is to do whatever you can to stay away from the word information. I suggest you use advice. No one has "advice overload."

Ask them for advice and it's like pointing a giant ray-gun at them that makes them start talking. My experience has been that almost universally, people will respond with "Sure thing. What's on your mind?" And then I'm off and running with them.

Asking for advice, beyond being very non-threatening, is a subtle way of showing a bit of well-placed deference. I am convinced that asking for advice has super powers. Give it a try. Swap out the information question for the "I was hoping you could give me some advice" strategy and see if you don't start getting warmer responses.

CHAPTER 7: Land Mine!

Handing Out To-Do's

In the years when I was in the marketing department, clawing my way up the corporate ladder, my life was dominated by a notebook. Several notebooks actually--they stacked up after a while. I would write my to-do list in these notebooks. I never made the jump to PDA light speed by taking notes on a Palm Pilot. I was always a notebook guy. I still am.

Anyway, there I'd sit in my office, doing whatever needed to be done at the time. Inevitably my phone would ring and sometimes it would be my beloved boss Spike. He would say on occasion "C'mon up. Bring your notebook."

And so I would. Nice to be needed actually. I'd plunk myself down in Spike's office and he'd assign eight or twelve to-do's to me. Spike was a great boss for a lot of reasons. One reason in particular was he was extremely organized. When he gave me my list of to-do's they would be in descending order of importance. No guesswork. Start at number one, Marty, and work your way down. I loved that guy.

Also, a lesson I learned from him was that he would be working from his own notebook in which he'd written his own list of to-do's he'd gotten from the President. The President probably got his from the Chairman. And this leads me to Bob Dylan.

Bob Dylan once sang "You've got to serve somebody" and even though Bob probably spent limited time in a corporate environment he sure was right.

Bob Dylan was saying that no matter who you are, somebody's going to your boss. Someone is going to be making demands of you. I made demands of my team. Spike made demands of me. The President made demands of Spike. Up the ladder it goes until you get to the Board of Directors who answer to the shareholders and investors.

Because my boss handed me to-do's left and right, what I didn't need was other people handing me a few more. And the same goes for Mr. Whizbang. Even if Mr. Whizbang is the end-all be-all in their organization, he or she has to serve somebody. No one is without to-do's. Rest assured that somewhere Mr. Whizbang's got his or her version of that notebook and the list of action items on its pages is as endless as mine and yours.

Leaving Mr. Whizbang a message that hands him or her another to-do, like "Please call me back" or "Please call me back with a time we can get together" or "Please call me back with the name of the person in your organization who…" is probably not a good idea. If you have not already established a relationship with Mr. Whizbang, handing him or her a to-do list is a bit presumptious.

And to my great astonishment nearly everyone does it. Who are we to give Mr. Whizbang a to-do? Mr. Whizbang doesn't serve us. Doesn't make sense.

This is a land mine of a most insidious nature. But I have studied it and I think I have it licked. The reason I had trouble figuring out how to avoid this land mine is that it is so enormously prevalent. This is a great way to set yourself apart. Get this land mine in your line of vision and never lose sight of it. That way, you won't be one of the incredible majority out there setting it off.

Avoiding the Handing Out To-Do's Land Mine

Ok, if you are serious about setting yourself apart by NOT triggering this land mine, here is how to do it.

Immediately remove the phrase "Please call me back" from your vocabulary. Do it. In your brain, highlight that phrase, press delete, and then empty your recycle bin so it's gone for good or at least out of reach.

Implicit in any voice mail message is a request for a call back, unless you specifically mention that no return call is needed. Handing Out To-Do's like "please call me back at..." is presumptuous and can be the harbinger of Wrath of The Rep (see Chapter 7).

When you leave someone a message, you are essentially parachuting into their day. One of my best friends, Dave, used to be in the military. His job while he served his country was to get in a perfectly good airplane, wait for it to get in the air and then jump out of it.

At night. At low altitude to avoid radar.

Dave said the reason for doing a parachute jump this way is to make sure that no one sees you coming. The Low Altitude Night Drop. Very effective. Keep in mind, Mr. Whizbang does not see your telephone call coming. He or she does not see your voice mail message in the distance as it flies through the fiber optic cables and reaches his or her mailbox. Every time you leave him or her an unexpected message you are pulling a "Low Altitude Night Drop." This is fine. It's the way business gets done. But don't step on a communication land mine and give Mr. Whizbang a to-do on top of it.

The Handing Out To-Do's land mine is not one of the more fatal communication errors in relation to some others. It is, however, insensitive and it is annoying. The perception held by some is that the higher you go in any business organization, the less those folks do. They are all high ranking corporate officers and as such, they have lots of time and not much to do. This is a giant misconception. It has been my experience that the folks at the very top of the corporate ladders are usually the busiest, most pressed-for-time people in the organizations.

I once worked for a company whose highest ranking executives all parked in a row right in front of the entrance to the building. On the nights when those folks had to work late, and there were many, all of us would walk by that row of cars on our way to our own. We were all going home but the officers of the company were staying. The higher you go, the busier they are. This is also true for owners of small businesses. They too are trying to get a million things done. They too have a notebook somewhere filled with to-do's. You may have the product or service that will help them get more done in less time. But if you hand them another to-do, make another demand of them, they may be less inclined to investigate it, or you.

Worth Repeating

❖ Even if Mr. Whizbang is the end-all be-all in their organization, he or she has to serve somebody. No one is without to-do's.

❖ The folks at the very top of the corporate ladders are usually the busiest, most pressed-for-time people in their organizations.

❖ Leaving Mr. Whizbang a message that hands him or her another to-do is probably not a good idea.

❖ Immediately remove the phrase "Please call me back" from your vocabulary.

Super Words and Phrases of Immeasurable Power
"You Don't Have to Chase Me"

The benefit of using this phrase is you won't get too upset when people don't call you back. When I call and leave a message I tell them straight up "… you don't have to chase me; I'll try to catch up with you later today/this week." It saves me a lot of grief. In my opinion it only makes sense. I can't expect someone to drop what they're doing because of my agenda. I do not think you can either.

If I leave ten messages in a day, I try to say this about eight times. This phrase has Super Power to be sure. It creates a few very good messages in the mind of Mr. Whizbang:

• I respect your time
• I'm an easy person with whom to do business
• I won't give you a hard time when you don't call me back

Of course, using this Phrase of Immeasurable Power puts the onus on you to follow up. But you were probably going to have to do that anyway.

This may be a coincidence but as soon as I incorporated this phrase into my everyday business life I began to get a few more call-backs. Not a huge increase but I noticed it. You may have the same result.

Also, and this is almost across the board, after leaving a "you don't have to chase me" message, I found that when I did get Mr. Whizbang on the phone, it was a much warmer call. Often a prospect will apologize for not getting back to me and I am always the model of accommodation because I let him or her off the hook immediately. This is critical because it is right here where you hit a conversational transition point. This is the point where the discussion of substance should begin. Moving through this transition with speed is essential. You definitely *do not* want to spend too much time at all on why Mr. Whizbang did not call you back. Even if Mr. Whizbang wants to explain, it is wise to get down to business as quickly as possible.

Try using this phrase for a day. How about a week? This tactic builds Whizbang loyalty and trust. There is an unmistakable air of common courtesy about incorporating this technique. And as you know there is very little less common than common courtesy. What better way to set yourself apart?

Section Two: E-mail

I love hockey pucks. Possibly the reason for this is because the entire game of hockey is devoted to the obsessive pursuit for possession of the puck so that it can be slammed into the net. A few years ago I had the great fortune to visit the Hockey Hall of Fame in Toronto, Canada. Right as you walk into the Hall of Fame there is a display of pucks through the ages. A giant wall of pucks. I stood there staring at the wall for minutes on end until one of my brothers noticed I was missing and came to wrest me away. Conversely, while playing in a hockey game I had the great *misfortune* of having my right eyebrow split open by a puck from an errant slap shot. Beyond being a bloody, messy affair, this was easily in the top five most painful events in my life.

So, used correctly, a puck can lead one to victory. Used carelessly, it can do some serious damage. This leads me to e-mail. E-mail is one of my favorite communication methods. I love e-mail. This is not to say I love all the e-mail messages that I get. Certainly not. I love e-mail as an entity, as a technology.

My great affection for e-mail does not however skew my opinion that electronic mail is easily one of the most abused communication mediums in the entire world of business. And I'm *not* talking about the volume of e-mail that flies around from day to day. No! No! No! The abuse to which I refer is the patent disregard the business world shows in failing to realize the power of this medium to damage one's professional image.

As much as the use of e-mail proliferates in the business world, so do the land mines involved with using it. Whenever somebody lays their hands on a keyboard and sends an e-mail message to someone, they display their ability or inability to communicate. E-mail forces the user into a position where he or she must communicate through the written word. And every e-mail message invites the world into the secret of how well or how poorly that person can write. Every time. And this has an enormous impact on what their cyber audience thinks of them.

There is also the added caveat that since e-mail messages often get forwarded, that writing ability or disability is often on display for more than just the folks who got the original message. I remember being in our president Rex's office when a conversation about an e-mail message broke out. We had been talking over some new product pricing, but Rex saw a paper on his desk and got derailed.

Rex: Mart. Mart. You know a guy named Darren? Down in Knoxville?

Marty: Um, I don't think Darren has had a chance to participate in any of the pricing –

Rex: Forget that a minute. Do you know the guy?

Marty: Well, uh, yeah. I was in Knoxville right at the beginning of the month. We were –

Rex: So you met the guy?

Marty: Well yes, of course. He's the manager.

Rex: Well he may be a manager but this kid's got a screw loose. Fay down in HR got this message and sent it on up to me for approval. Look at this thing, man. It's what, two and a half pages, it's got typos all over it, and I can't figure out what the guy wants. Here.

Marty: (reading) I think he's making a case for adding two more sales people. But, true, he's a little all over the place and –

Rex: A little? A little? I've read bowls of alphabet soup that made more sense than that.

Marty: (still reading) --and, of course, there is no semicolon in the word 'territory.' Why'd you print this out?

Rex: Because I want to show it to his boss and ask him why his managers have no communication skills. Mart, if he's sending that to Fay, what's he sending out to customers? Think about it.

Dangerous, no? Yes, very dangerous. The fact that e-mail messages can and do get forwarded should be enough incentive for everyone in the global business community to watch out for the land mines that populate the e-mail communication method. But land mines are going off left and right, every day, through business people's disastrous e-mail skills.

Here's another example: I have no idea how I got on this distribution list but I get a weekly, *weekly* newsletter sent to my inbox. As soon as I see it I delete it not only because I never signed up for it but because it is almost always a huge amount of text. I once copied the document into a word processing program and then hit the "word count" button to see how many words this person had dumped into the message. The number came back 1,378 words. 1,378? In one message? An electronic newsletter? What a disaster.

And while that may be an extreme example of someone stomping on a communication land mine, it is a fact that while the business world has jumped on the e-mail bandwagon, it hasn't taken the time to learn, or re-learn, some of the rudimentary rules of written communication. And they go about doing themselves damage every day.

Imagine that automobiles had been invented only a few years ago and they were as easily and cheaply acquired as an e-mail address and Internet access are today. What would happen? Everyone would get themselves a car, jump in and start zooming around without ever having learned how to drive. There would be millions of cars out there smashing into one another, smashing into stationary objects, and generally making the roadways an extremely dangerous place.

Keep that picture in your mind every time you fire up your computer and open your e-mail program because that is *exactly* what has happened. Everyone has e-mail capability, but precious few are paying attention to any of the guidelines of proper and effective written communication. Because of this, e-mail is a treacherous communication method, fraught with all kinds of ways to do yourself professional damage.

And this is very good news.

For you.

The good news is that very few business professionals monitor how they are coming across in e-mail. As a result, with very little effort you can set yourself apart. Mr. Whizbang receives e-mail messages that are long winded, difficult to follow, and have little or no command of the

English language. Mr. Whizbang's reaction to these is like anyone else's reaction, he or she lowers his or her opinion of the message's sender.

Mr. Whizbang also receives e-mail messages that are pithy, compelling, and display an admirable ability to communicate. Mr. Whizbang's opinion of the sender may or may not be raised by these types of messages, but at least the sender hasn't done any damage to their professional image.

Some of the most common and most damaging e-mail land mines are outlined in this section. Keep them in mind every time you touch a keyboard, and you will begin to distinguish yourself from the rest of the e-mailers out there smashing into things and denting their professional images.

The advent and mass adoption of e-mail has brought the written word back into the mainstream. So you can choose to develop your writing skills or continue to trip e-mail land mines like everyone else.

CHAPTER 8: Land Mine!

The Term Paper

Waaaaaay back when I was attending my beloved alma mater, Lafayette College, I majored in English. And even though my academic performance at Lafayette would charitably be described as marginal, I was always pretty enthusiastic about being an English major. I suspect the faculty recognized this, gave me a break here and there, and I graduated on time and all that.

I realize now that my major actually proved to be excellent business training for me, though I did not appreciate this, or much else, at the time. English majors write lots of papers. It's how the faculty finds out what you know and whether or not you can be articulate about it. And because I wrote a lot of papers, a common experience of mine throughout college was receiving the pity of others who would voice sympathetic comments like:

"A paper? On a *book*? Oh man, I could never do that. No way. If I had to write more than like a few pages I think I'd like lose it or whatever. Better you than me."

Possibly I am indulging my own paranoid sense of conspiracy here, but it is my belief that these same "term-paper phobic" people are the ones who churn out these monster e-mail Term Papers today. They clutter cyber inboxes with giant, sprawling notations that mire their points in a fetid morass of unnecessary words.

Regardless of who sends them, the Term Papers are out there. The huge e-mail message. The "How Long Am I Going Have to Scroll Down to Get to the End of this Thing" e-mail message. The Term Paper. Fear it.

I've been a fan of "Saturday Night Live" since it started in 1975. When my parents went out on Saturday nights my two older brothers would let me stay up with them to watch the show. I was a big fan of the Coneheads. True, they were fun to look at, but what delighted me more than that were the ways the Coneheads would use long, unnecessarily complicated descriptions to communicate everyday things to each other.

For example, when a Conehead said he was eating "small starch tubes combined with lactate extract of hoofed mammals," it meant macaroni and cheese was for dinner. When a Conehead said she was attending "a voluntary gathering of humans to absorb sound patterns," it meant she was going to a rock concert.

Communicating like a Conehead on a comedy television show is extremely entertaining. Communicating like a Conehead in an e-mail message puts you in land mine city.

You've gotten them. Possibly you've sent an e-mail treatise or two yourself. E-mail Term Papers are pretty common, so don't be ashamed. The e-mail Term Paper is the e-mail message that, regardless of subject matter, is just a long, tired dissertation that would make even Alexander Dumas[1] say "Whoa! That's a lot of text. What a nightmare." Even if it's a *riveting* dissertation, it's still an e-mail land mine.

---

[1]Alexander Dumas wrote, among others, *The Three Musketeers* and *The Count of Monte Cristo.* These novels were first published as "serials" in the newspaper. The newspaper paid Alexander by the line so his stories tended to be rather lengthy. Spellbinding, but lengthy. These books are huge. My copy of *The Count of Monte Cristo* is 1,136 pages long. Great book. You ought to read it.

Keep in mind that e-mail is essentially a speed medium. Communicating through e-mail buys you incredible speed. And this speed exists on both sides of the communication. You as the sender compose what you want to say, attach what you consider to be important, and hit "send." Wham! The hubs, routers, fiber, and whatever else they have out there in the ethosphere deliver your message to Mr. Whizbang's desktop in seconds. Sometimes your message even comes with a pleasant "ping" sound to alert Mr. Whizbang that he or she has an important message waiting.

Whether Mr. Whizbang is a prospect, your Boss, or whoever, Mr. Whizbang is moving quickly and will not, I promise you, stop to read every word of your giant e-mail message. If it is of absolute necessity Mr. Whizbang may print it out and read it later. But most times he or she will keep moving right past it.

Beyond a missed opportunity to get your point(s) across, what impressions have you left on Mr. Whizbang by burdening him or her with this mammoth message? If you answer that Mr. Whizbang now thinks you are longwinded, you do not communicate well, and you do not respect his or her time, then you are correct. Even if this is not an accurate picture of you, this is the impression you are creating in Mr. Whizbang's mind. This is not good at all.

I once received an e-mail Term Paper from a sales rep we will, for the purposes of this story, refer to as Cosmo. Cosmo was trying to introduce me to a software package that would help me track, estimate the cost of, and report on many separate projects at one time. Nifty. For someone heading up both the Marketing and Training departments of a mid-sized company, this could come in handy. Through the due diligence of his homework, Cosmo found out who I was and got my e-mail address.

As you can see, Cosmo did just fine during the initial phase of the process. However Cosmo then proceeded to send me an e-mail message that was four and a half pages long. I was absolutely amazed. And irritated. Did this kid really think I was going to bring my day to screeching halt and read his dissertation?

He had cut and pasted sections off his company's Web site that explained the entire suite of services. Cosmo made comments on each section, explaining how this was going to make me more productive, happy, and successful.

Wanting to use this message as a teaching point I immediately sent it out to my team with a note asking simply "Any comments?" This was a mistake. An uproar ensued. Pandemonium exploded on the 8th floor. A line formed at my door. Apparently my team felt that I was asking them not only to read word for word Cosmo's e-mail, but also to make sense of it and report on what they thought of it. This would have easily killed all of their week-ends. My team was in revolt. A leader was elected. The leader of the Rebellion was a young lady who was a particular favorite of mine owing to her cool head and her uncanny ability to meet unreasonable deadlines. Her parents had named her after one of our own 50 states. And while her actual name is a perfectly nice name I must change it now, for the purposes of this story, to Delaware.

Delaware knocked as she walked into my office and stood directly in front of my desk. The following conversation ensued:

Delaware: Mart, what's up with this e-mail? Do you want us to break it down right now or can we take the weekend?

Marty: E-mail?

Delaware: The e-mail you sent. You *just* sent. From some guy named Cosmo.

Marty: I sent it or Cosmo sent it?

Delaware: You *forwarded* it. Cosmo wrote it, whoever Cosmo is. Apparently he has a lot to say. You sent it to the whole team. What are we supposed to do with this thing? It's gotta be like 50 pages long.

Marty: What's all the noise in the hall? And as you know, there are smoke alarms all over this building, so could you take a leadership position for me and tell the team to extinguish those torches. And where did they get the pitchforks?

Delaware: Mart... MART! I have the Site Seller to finish, Doris is completely underwater with the database, and Gwen over in Graphics—

Marty: Oh I do love Gwen.

Delaware: --is supposed to leave for a week in *Maine* tonight. Mart, what do you want done with this thing?

Marty: You are trying to destroy me.

Delaware: Mart, you gotta focus here.

Marty: Why are you trying to destroy me? I am Tokyo and you are Godzilla. You are trying to destroy me.

Delaware: Mart! Have you *read* that e-mail? I'm surprised it didn't crash the entire network. There's probably people in Information Services right now trying to hang themselves with their belts.

Marty: This is about that e-mail I sent, isn't it?

At this point, my beloved Delaware gave up, sat down and put her forehead down on my desk.

I calmly explained to Delaware that I was merely hoping to use Cosmo's message as an example of how *not* to communicate and that everyone's weekend was safe. Delaware was most relieved and left my office to relay this information to the rest of the rioting villagers. The uprising quelled, we all went back to work. By the way, Cosmo's e-mail message got printed out somewhere and posted on the soda machine on our floor as a symbol of e-mail ineptitude.

Later that week, Cosmo left me a voice mail message, "Hi Mr. Clarke, this is Cosmo from Software Company. I'm just following up on an e-mail I sent you and I wanted to see if we could set up a time when we could get together and discuss it. ..."

Now you tell me, how inclined was I to give Cosmo an appointment? Exactly, not very. Neither would you. Cosmo did serious damage to my impression of him simply by stepping on the Term Paper land mine.

Avoiding the Term Paper Land Mine

Again, keep present in your mind at all times that e-mail is a speed medium. It can move ideas around at an incredible pace. I began my business career before e-mail exploded on the scene and I still wonder how we ever got along without it. Fast, reliable, and economical, e-mail is a huge communication force in our professional lives. When you craft an e-mail message, you must do everything in your power to avoid anything that impedes the speed at which your points, ideas, and suggestions get communicated. Next time you send a message of any importance at all, give these ideas a try:

The Subject Line

If you can communicate your message within the confines of the Subject Line, do it. For example, if you are confirming an appointment with Mr. Whizbang it is entirely acceptable to write "Thursday, 11:15am is confirmed. Thanks!" in the subject line. The first time you do it, Mr. Whizbang is going to check the e-mail message anyway to see if that was all you had to say. Finding nothing there and realizing that you are the model of economy, he or she won't do it a second time. And he or she will appreciate your making life just a bit simpler

The Post–it® Note

I have a few heroes in my life. Art Fry is one of them.

Art Fry dreamed of turning his simple invention into a bigger success. He wanted to help himself to his dream, but he wanted his dream to help others. Do you know Art Fry? I'll bet you've used his invention. That's right. He is the 3M Corporation engineer who invented Post-it® Notes. Here's how he turned his dream into a reality. While singing in his church choir, he kept losing his place in the hymnal, because his bookmark kept slipping out of sight. He used the bookmarks to help ease the chore of finding the next song to be sung. He tried folding the page edges, but that tactic didn't work either. The other choir members expressed similar concerns. His frustration drove him to do what he does best – practical chemical engineering. Art came up with a bookmark that had a patch of stickum on one side. His idea worked so well that soon all the other choir members wanted sticky bookmarks. Art decided to look for other applications, and created stickum notepads. The secretarial pool loved his notepads, and so did hundreds of 3M employees. Eventually 3M built a multi-billion dollar business out of Art Fry's multi colored Post-it® Notes.

It is my opinion that if one were to remove all the Post-it® Notes from Corporate America, the economic systems of the world would implode instantaneously. Think of a world without Post-It Notes... No, it is too horrifying.

If you have an e-mail message to send and you are afraid it may turn out to be a Term Paper here's a trick: Get out a regulation sized, square Post-it® Note. Use whichever color you like. Color does not matter, size matters. A regulation Post-it® Note covers the palm of your hand. These days you can get Post-it® Notes the size of a swimming pool, which, for a body of water is actually not that big, but for a Post-it® Note is rather large. Just get a regular square Post-it® Note and use it to summarize your ideas.

If you can summarize your ideas on that Post-it® Note, then you can stick it to your monitor and type away. This may sound lame, the idea of sticking a Post-it® Note on your monitor, *preparing* yourself to send an e-mail message. Well, then it's lame. Lame and smart. Ten seconds of prep to decide what you want to say is actually not that big a price to pay in order to set yourself apart as an effective communicator. If it's lame then I'm lame because I use this technique two or three times a week.

Keep in mind, this technique is not a foolproof method to avoid the Term Paper land mine. It is entirely possible to fit your ideas neatly on a Post-it® Note and then go ahead and send out some huge monster document.

If by chance your summary *cannot* fit on the Post-it® Note, then you definitely have a Term Paper on your hands. You, my friend, are standing directly on the Term Paper land mine. But it hasn't gone off. You can save yourself (and Mr. Whizbang) quite easily. Here's what you can do: in either in the subject line or, if you must, in the body section of the e-mail message write "My (insert appropriate descriptor) is attached." Then open up your word processing program of preference, write your message, and send your document as an attachment. You have just avoided a land mine.

Almost.

> *A word about attachments. Now who knew this one was going to be such a flashpoint of controversy? A while back I was giving a speech to a perfectly normal and well-behaved corporate audience and the topic of attachments came up. A debate broke out immediately, a few people were for attachments and a few people hated them and the people who sent them. Things got heated up and before I knew it I had a prison riot on my hands.*
>
> *I played the fence-sitting mediator that day (I didn't want to get beaned with a date book) and I survived that hullabaloo. However it occurs to me that I need to take a definite stand on attachments and their applications. I feel attachments are absolutely acceptable. Attachments come in all shapes and sizes these days. They are a necessary and good business tool.*

Sending a document of any length as an attachment without any explanation is a bit like throwing the entire Sunday paper at Mr. Whizbang's door and then pedaling away. It lacks professional courtesy. So, in order to make life easy for Mr. Whizbang SUMMARIZE your document in the body section of the message. A summary is the best friend of the attachment-sending e-mailer.

Be advised, according to the Martin Academy of Mathematics there is *nothing* that cannot be summarized. I know, it's a bold statement. Even though I am a liberal arts major born into a family of MIT engineers (can you imagine?), I feel this is a mathematical certainty – there is no topic that cannot be summarized. Watch:

The World: Everyone lives there

The Toronto Maple Leafs: Hockey team

My Mom: Wonderful woman. Librarian. Bought me Springsteen tickets in 1983.

Death: On its way but probably not right this second.

These are non business-related examples; however, the following e-mail example will illustrate my point as it relates to business. It's a simple e-mail message from a wise employee named Joe Bergen to his boss's boss, Mr. Whizbang:

Subject: As requested: My Virtual Site
Seller Idea

Mr. Whizbang,
The attached document details my idea for a Virtual Site Seller for our sales force. In it you will find:
* *What a Virtual Site Seller is*
* *Why a Virtual Site Seller will increase sales*
* *What costs are involved*
* *Time frames*

I will not move forward without your edits and approvals.

Thanks,
Joe Bergen

I can tell you Mr. Whizbang is loving Joe Bergen. Oh, the glory of a nice summary. How polished, how very professional. Nice second effort. Well done, my excellent friend.

Bullets, Bullets, Bullets!

I write paragraphs for a living. I love paragraphs. Paragraphs are good, paragraphs are our friend. There are many paragraphs in this very book. Perhaps I snuck a few by you. But even having said that, I will say with absolute certainty that writing paragraphs is a dangerous practice in the modern medium of electronic mail. Why? Because we live in a "bullet world."

Figure out how to establish a bulleted list in your e-mail program and do not be afraid to use that function. Let's say Joe Bergen is sending an e-mail message out to 12 people, explaining the agenda and particulars for a special meeting. Compare and contrast:

Example 1:

The Virtual Site Seller meeting will be held on Tuesday, October 14th at 9:30am in the Berkley conference room. We'll try to cover the purpose of and the text requirements of the Virtual Site Seller as well as who can contribute to the various sections including install procedures, customer care, and the escalation list. One of the things we're trying to accomplish is to have everyone take away a list of action items that will remain open until our project manager, Dominick D'Orazio checks them off. Keep in mind that we want to move quickly in this meeting to respect everyone's time, so please bring a list of essential contacts to this meeting so we can begin to form a list for our sales force.

Joe Bergen
Extension 112

Example 2:

Hi folks, if you're reading this you are invited!

Purpose: The Virtual Site Seller Meeting
Date: Tuesday, October 14
Time: 9:15am
Place: Berkley Conference Room
Project Leader: Joe Bergen, Ext 112
Project Manager: Dominick D'Orazio, Ext 777
Tentative agenda:
- *Virtual Site Seller requirements*
- *Section needs*
- *Special attention*
  o Install
  o Customer Care
  o Escalation
- *Assignment of Action Items*
- *Special Guests – The Web-Enabler team from Information Systems*

See you there!

Perhaps you do not see a difference. If that is the case let me make the suggestion that you find the deepest, most mysterious and frightening lake closest to your actual position, go to its shores, and cast this book far into its deepest waters.

If you do see a difference, then the point is clear. A bulleted summary is infinitely better than a paragraph. This is a painful admission coming from a man who loves the idea, the concept of a paragraph. What can I tell you? Business is business, and e-mail is different from writing books. Find out how to establish bullets on your computer and use that capability as much as you can.

The Scroll Box is Your Friend

In most word processing and e-mail programs, a scroll bar appears on the right side of one's document. The scroll bar contains a little square or rectangle, called a scroll box or slider, that moves up and down to mark where you are relative to the entire document or message. Show a little respect. This is an enormously valuable and practical icon.

The scroll box has an interesting attribute: the little square gets smaller in direct proportion to the length of your document. This is key! If the scroll bar never appears, that means the text of your document can be contained in the natural window of the average person's computer screen. This is your goal. However, if after you are finished typing your e-mail the scroll box has withered down to a tiny sliver, back away from the "send" button. *Anytime* Mr. Whizbang has to scroll you're in trouble. If you write an e-mail message that makes Mr. Whizbang scroll, it better be good.

Pay attention to the scroll bar, particularly to the size and shape of the scroll box. At first it's a rectangle. Then it's a square. Then it's a considerably smaller rectangle. It gets smaller as your document gets larger. Keep an eye on it. If you use e-mail to get your message across, you would do well to avoid the microscopic rectangle to which an e-mail term paper reduces the scroll box.

Worth Repeating

❖ Keep in mind that e-mail is essentially a speed medium.

❖ When you craft an e-mail message, you must do everything in your power to avoid anything that impedes the speed at which your points, ideas, and suggestions get communicated.

❖ If you can communicate your message within the confines of the Subject Line, do it.

❖ If your summary cannot fit on a Post-it® Note, then you definitely have a Term Paper on your hands.

❖ Ten seconds of prep, deciding what you want to say is actually not that big a price to pay in order to set yourself apart as an effective communicator.

❖ We live in a "bullet world."

❖ If you write an e-mail message that makes Mr. Whizbang scroll, it better be good.

Super Words and Phrases of Immeasurable Power

"Tight Fit"

I use "Tight Fit" in e-mail as well as on the phone and face-to-face. This is a phrase that you can use at the critical and oftentimes awkward time when you need to suggest that Mr. Whizbang should consider hiring you, donating to your charity, giving you an appointment, or whatever critical action Mr. Whizbang needs to take for you to be successful in your particular endeavor. There comes a time in most business exchanges when you need to push Mr. Whizbang in that direction. This pushing must be done professionally and with respect. Here are a few examples of how the phrase "tight fit" can work to your advantage.

If I want to gain an appointment with Mr. Whizbang I would try to work in something along the lines of:

"I was hoping you and I could sit down together and see if there is a tight fit between what we offer and what you are trying to accomplish at Whizbang Inc. Can we meet briefly at 10 AM on the 15th?"

I've asked for the appointment in a professional way and made it very easy for Mr. Whizbang to say "yes." All we are going to do is see if there is a "tight fit" between our two companies. This is extremely non-threatening.

A way to turn this phrase a bit more aggressively is to say:

"I've done some research on Whizbang Inc and I think there is more than one way we can be a tight fit for your organization. I was hoping to get on your schedule on the 15th at 10 AM to sit down with you and hear your opinion on it."

Sometimes this phrase can be useful in a closing situation. Let's say you are in a job interview and the time comes to ask for the job.

"Mr. Whizbang, from what we've talked about today, I am of the opinion that I would be a very tight fit for Whizbang Inc. If you share that opinion, I think we should pick a start date."

Everyone understands the colloquialism "tight fit." It is a wonder of economy. In two words it paints an emotional picture of something that works just great and certainly feels right. That is a picture worth painting in the mind of Mr. Whizbang.

CHAPTER 9: Land Mine!

Grammar and Spelling

I have some very bad news. Grammar is back. So is spelling. Blame electronic mail, blame what you like but the truth of the matter is that grammar and spelling are back.

I have heard the argument, "Mart, that's preposterous, Mr. Whizbang either doesn't know much about grammar or doesn't care when it's in an e-mail message. Paying attention to grammar and spelling is a waste of time."

I disagree entirely.

Why do most people accept the fact that a typo on your resume can cost you a job opportunity, but grammar and spelling don't count when you use e-mail? My theory is the massive volume of e-mail messages that most business professionals send and receive has desensitized them. Because of the volume of e-mail and the incredible speed at which we are all forced to work, the assumption has become that it is OK to be a little sloppy. Volume and speed makes sloppy acceptable. Again, I disagree. Leave sloppy for the masses.

"I send so *many* messages, they don't all have to be well-written, do they?"

Why not? Being well-written implies neither complexity nor length. Bullets can be well-written or poorly written just as sentences can. Writing well is an excellent way to set yourself apart. And you do not have to be Webster or Shake-

111

speare to avoid a few of the mini grammar and spelling land mines that plague the e-mail landscape. It is very easy. There is no need for us all to stop what we're doing and start diagramming sentences.

Poor grammar and spelling are going to hurt your professional image. Poor writing skills send Mr. Whizbang the message that you are either sloppy or ignorant. Or both. These are not the adjectives you want popping into Mr. Whizbang's head when he or she reads your e-mail message.

Think about your shoes. In any business setting there is no guarantee that Mr. Whizbang will take note of your shoes. If he or she does, it may not be a deal-breaker if your shoes are unpolished and slightly threadbare. However, an impression is made and that impression may be negative. Setting yourself apart *in a good way* is the goal. The point is to set yourself apart, and *not* to be lumped in with everybody else. Why not have nice shoes on? It is relatively easy to do, all it requires is a little effort. Not paying attention to your spelling and grammar is just as sloppy.

One of the worst impressions that can be created in the mind of Mr. Whizbang is that you have a low score in the "Pays Attention to Details" category. When you have spelling errors and grammatical mistakes all over the place, you flirt with creating that very impression.

Attention to detail is a huge issue. If Mr. Whizbang ever gets the idea that you are sloppy with details, that perception can very well be a deal breaker. Think about this: would you use an auto mechanic with a reputation for not paying attention to detail? How about a dentist? How about a contractor to build your house? If Mr. Whizbang feels you have a low attention-to-detail score, the chances of him or her doing business with you is extremely low. And that is exactly the message poor grammar and spelling sends to Mr. Whizbang.

The number and variety of grammar and spelling land mines out there is nearly limitless. However, through my tenure in Corporate America a few have become favorite targets of mine owing to the amazing regularity with which they get detonated.

If you learn to avoid just these few, you will not only set yourself apart, you will also gain more confidence every time you sit at your keyboard and rap out nice well written-message to Mr. Whizbang.

Avoiding the Grammar and Spelling Land Mine

Spelling

> *Spell check is your enemy.*
> --M. Clarke

Oh, it is so true. Spell check is the sworn enemy of the business communicator. It's fake, it's a scam. The spell check function is NOT a security blanket, a safety net, or some virtual spelling insurance policy.

"Did you send that e-mail?"

"Yes."

"Did you review it before you sent it?"

"I spell checked it."

Wrong wrong wrong!

Wait, let me pause to make an analogy before I get myself all worked up.

In the western part of Florida, connecting the towns of St. Petersburg and Bradenton, is a bridge called the Sunshine Skyway. The Sunshine Skyway is roughly a trillion miles long and rises 12 million feet high over Tampa Bay. Actually that's not true, but it feels that way when you drive over it. That thing punches quite a hole in the skyline.

There are guard rails that line each side of the Sunshine Skyway to help drivers stay on the road and *not* plunge headlong off the bridge. Otherwise motorists might plummet to violent and terrifying deaths.

But even though these guard rails are there, most drivers keep their eyes wide open while driving along the Sunshine Skyway. No one says, "Oh look! Guardrails! Excellent. I'll take my eyes off the road and read a magazine while I drive over to Bradenton." That would be stupid in the extreme.

So is relying entirely on a spell checking engine to protect you from spelling mistakes. The spell checking engine is to your e-mail message as the guard rails are to the Sunshine Skyway. Nice to have but you still have to pay attention.

One thing I will say for spell check, it knows that "heighth" is not a word. And it's not. No matter how many people insist on using it, "heighth" is not a word.

Wide is a word.

Width is a word.

Height is a word.

"Heighth" is *not* a word.

The following sentence is correct:

"Today we will discuss the height and width of Henrik Ibsen's bookshelves."

That is a correct sentence and the portent of a barn-burner of a discussion.

Every time I read "heighth" in a message (or worse, hear it in a conversation) it goes into my head and rattles the fillings in my teeth. I once sat in our president's "Private Conference Room" with six other Execs while we discussed some live event we were going to stage for the employees. It was murder hearing one of the execs wield "heighth" around like a blunt instrument. I could have easily interrupted the man and explained that "heighth" was not a word in his or anyone else's native language, but it wasn't the hill I wanted to die on that day so I suffered in silence.

So I'll say that much for spell check, but it is still your enemy.

Grammar

The "rules" of English grammar are the subject of heated debate. What is a rule and what is not? What rules are hopelessly outdated? Are there exceptions to the rules? Who is making these rules? The war over what is and what is not "correct" rages on, and I hope it always will, because I find the debate most entertaining. But, getting down to the business of being well written, here are my top three grammar land mines. Avoid these and you'll be head and shoulders above 90% of your peers.

1. *Ending a Sentence with a Preposition*

A simple switch usually cures this one:
Wrong: What room are you going to?
Right: To what room are you going?
Wrong: What day are we meeting on?
Right: On what day are we meeting?

Sometimes, prepositions just get tacked on to sentences for no apparent reason.

Wrong: Where is that town at?
Right: Where is that town?

In these cases, just leave off the preposition and you will avoid sounding like an uneducated pinhead.

Once you get a feel for how prepositions work in sentences, you can begin to spot the times when you are ending a sentence with one.

2.   *Who and Whom*

Figuring out whether who or whom is correct in any given situation can be difficult. The fact that who is normally the subject of a verb and whom is usually the object of a verb is true but not typically helpful. Here's a method that works most of the time for me: anytime I use the word "he" I usually go with "who." Anytime I use the word "him" I go with "whom."

Let's use this sentence to illustrate:

"Let's give the money to the person (who or whom) needs it the most."

At this point a dialogue goes on in my head which helps me fit "he" or "him" in the sentence and see what sounds right.

What sounds right, "he needs it the most" or "him needs it the most"? Clearly "he" sounds correct and so I'd go with "who" in that situation.

Here is another one:

"With (who or whom) are you meeting tomorrow?"

Again, I'd try the sentence using "him" or "he."

"Are you meeting with he tomorrow?" No, that doesn't sound right, does it?

"Are you meeting with him tomorrow?" That sounds correct. In the case where "him" sounds right I use "whom." Works like a charm.

3.   *Split Infinitives*

I see split infinitives everywhere. I see them on Web sites, in e-mail messages, in letters, and I see them in press releases. Press releases! How can a corporate press release get approved when it contains one of the most basic grammatical errors in the history of the language? This baffles me. But I see split infinitives every day.

Some folks say that splitting infinitives is perfectly fine in this day and age. I am not in league with these people. In casual conversation, split infinitives are no crime. But when you are writing a letter or an e-mail message to Mr. Whizbang, split infinitives are sloppy. The good news is they are extremely easy to avoid. Let's start with a definition:

An infinitive is the combination of the word "to" and then the verb itself. For example:

-to feel
-to be
-to eat
-to have
-to suffer
-to win
-to look

All these are perfectly nice infinitives. In a sentence they can look like this:

"It is important to be prepared at all times."
"We want to feel better about this situation."
"They need to meet quickly and get this thing settled."

See? Nice, nice, nice. Each of these infinitives is as clean as a whistle. All this about split infinitives, much ado about nothing. A tempest in a tea cup, no?

No. The split infinitive is everywhere. Even though it ought to be easy enough to avoid, it's all over the place. Here's the point, when one puts a word, any word, in between the "to" and the verb, one has split an infinitive. Let's turn those examples around and do them all wrong by splitting infinitives. (This pains me by the way.)

"It is important *to always be* prepared."
"We want *to really feel* better about this situation."
"They need *to quickly meet* and get this thing settled."
"*To boldly go* where no man has gone before."

Bad, bad, bad. Each one of these sentences has a split infinitive in it.

Do large sales, promotions, or the Iditarod hinge on avoiding these grammar and spelling land mines? No. But if you are going to lay your hands on a keyboard, why not take a minimal amount of care and produce something a bit more polished?

Worth Repeating

❖ Grammar is back. So is spelling.
❖ Being well-written is an excellent way to set yourself apart.
❖ Poor writing skills send Mr. Whizbang the message that you are either sloppy or ignorant. Or both.
❖ Attention to detail is a huge issue. If Mr. Whizbang ever gets the idea that you are sloppy with details, that idea can very well be a deal breaker.
❖ Spell check is your enemy.
❖ "Heighth" is not a word.
❖ Do not end sentences with prepositions.
❖ Learn when to use Who and when to use Whom.
❖ Do not split infinitives

Super Words and Phrases of Immeasurable Power

"Curious"

I learned the word "Curious" has super powers from my boss Spike. Working for Spike was one of the most enjoyable and valuable professional experiences I've ever had. I learned quite a few things from Spike, and this is just one of them. And even though it is pretty subtle, it remains a particular favorite of mine.

If you were on Spike's staff, you lived in a walled city where Spike was the supreme ruler and amused himself by heaping good-natured abuse on you almost constantly. In fact, the more abuse you got, the more you knew you were on Spike's good side. There was an upside to living inside the walled city, and that was Spike was the only one who was allowed to abuse you. If you were on Spike's staff, you didn't have to take any garbage from anyone else. Spike was fiercely protective of us.

Spike's bad side was actually quite plain. The infrequent visit to Spike's bad side was tolerated, but if you made a habit of it you simply disappeared from the company's organizational chart. I knew this, and fortunately I identified a few very distinct and consistent clues that would tell me if I was in the crosshairs of Spike's quiet fury

1.My Name

In private, Spike usually addressed me as Sweetheart, Chowder Head, or Dork. There were others, all colorful and inventive trust me, but decorum must carry the day and I will not articulate them here. All the names Spike used were welcome signs of his affection. It was when he would use my first name to me that the red flags started showing up. For instance if I picked up my phone and heard "Hey, Loser, it's Spike. Get up here." I knew I was fine. But if I heard "Marty, come on up to my office when you get a minute" I would search my mind for the sins of my past and try to outguess him because my first name meant I was no longer the Golden Boy. In fact, I might be the Gone Boy.

2. The word "concerned"

This one was simple. I heard this word used three times during my stretch with Spike and each time the person whose name was mentioned in the same sentence with "concerned" disappeared within two weeks. If Spike ever describes his feelings for you as concerned, my advice would be to go on down to HR and get a few nice boxes and pack up your office. Saves time.

3. The word "curious"

"Curious" was the one Spike would use to get your attention in a conversation. It worked like a charm. Typically, if I were sitting across from Spike and he started out with "Hey, about the Lexicom account. I'm curious..." that meant that Spike suspected I had dropped the ball on something but before he rained fire on me he wanted to get his facts straight.

The word "curious" is an excellent word to add to your professional vocabulary because it's not commonly heard in business exchanges and it carries with it a sense of thoughtfulness. Given these two characteristics, it has the power to make Mr. Whizbang lean a little forward toward you. Using this word, even casually, is a Whizbang attention getter.

Putting the phrase, "Mr. Whizbang, I'm curious..." at the beginning of any interrogative statement gives you license to ask nearly anything. Curious is especially useful as an introduction to a delicate question. For example, let's say you suspect the person across the desk from you is actually not the real Mr. Whizbang and you want to ask a question that will tell you if your suspicions are correct. This is thin ice to be sure because there are more than a few ways to insult someone while trying to find out if they are actually Mr. Whizbang.

The ham-handed approach usually follows the thinly veiled lines of "So, is anyone else involved with making this decision?" The more artful way to approach this might be, "Mr. Whizbang, I'm curious about the decision process and I was hoping you could help clarify a few things for me." Again, using curious implies you have given the question some prior thought, which will cause Mr. Whizbang to be that much more receptive to hearing your question and then replying in kind with a thoughtful, more detailed answer.

CHAPTER 10: Land Mine!

Emotional E-mail

So there you are at a hockey game. You are most pleased. The bright white ice. The players. The puck. The high speed, willful collision of really big guys.

There you are, and you notice that the game has become very tense. Tempers are running high and players are beginning to use their sticks as weapons a bit more than is usually acceptable. When this starts happening you can note it by remarking, out loud:

"Whoa, sticks are coming up out there."

Yes, it is a fact of hockey life, sometimes things get tense and "sticks come up."

"Sticks come up" in business too. It has been my experience that the world of business is populated by people who have a very deep passion for what they are trying to accomplish. Drivers. Ramrods. Type A's. Self-starters. Positive thinkers. Go-getters. Rah rahs. Whatever. Call them what you like, these people have their hearts in it.

I love business people for this very reason. These folks have a passion for their work. And in my experience, once in a while, in the course of getting things done, sometimes tempers flare and "sticks come up."

Certainly it is not an every day or even an every month thing. But it happens. Some friction is natural. In my opinion, civilized conflict is actually a good thing. But conflict situations are fraught with land mines and one of the most common outcomes from a "sticks come up" situation occurs when somebody writes an e-mail message when he or she is in an emotionally upset state.

I'm not Henry Ford but I've been in business long enough to say that I have never, *never* seen an Emotional E-Mail message do anyone any good. The recipients usually react negatively to a flaming e-mail message and the author is never cast in a positive light. In fact, I've seen some serious career damage done to a few folks who have fired off this type of e-mail message. No matter how "in the right" they may have been, the damage got done and it wound up being self-inflicted.

Tripping the Emotional E-Mail land mine can end a career, irreparably tarnish a reputation, and precipitate the odd crying jag. This story is simple enough and illustrates how a single bad piece of judgment caused a nasty mess. I call this story

The Executive Director, the Article, and the Cash Cow

Way up in the hinterlands of Connecticut there is a Community Theatre that for the purposes of this story we'll name the Kieran Center for the Arts. This is a very upscale community theatre dedicated to bringing to the stage a wide variety of high class art, music, and theatrical drama.

If you know anything about community theatres, you know that a steady stream of money needs to exist, pouring into the theatres' accounts. Ticket sales do not cut it, trust me. The funds typically come from some extremely well-off donors who are either civic-minded corporations or families who have that kind of money lying around. Behind every nice community theatre there exist many, or at the very least one giant, cash cow.

The Kieran Center was no exception. Their cash cow was the Sherwood family. Holy smokes did these folks have a ton of money. The entire family couldn't spend the interest on the interest. They just loved the folks at the Kieran Center and had made many generous donations to the Theatre. Generous in the sense that the check required a few commas. But to their credit, the Sherwood family was extremely quiet about their financial involvement because they were strictly of the opinion that supporting the arts has absolutely *nothing* to do with publicity. They had a low opinion of the press and kept themselves quite clear of it.

The Executive Director of the Kieran Center was a man we'll call Edward. Edward was not a small-minded man. But Edward had a small-minded moment, acted upon it and unfortunately all it bought him was a big mess.

All of us get angry from time to time. We all have small-minded moments. I have them all the time, mostly when I'm driving. To have a small-minded moment and keep it to yourself is acceptable. To act on it is often where people blow themselves up. As I said, unfortunately Edward acted on it.

A nice publicity article extolling the success of the Kieran Center appeared in the Connecticut Arts magazine. There were plenty of spiffy pictures and glowing text about the Theater. This article was written and then placed in the magazine by the Public Relations manager, Cammi. The article made no mention of the Sherwood family and all was well, except that the article also made no mention of the Center's top dog, the man with the plan, Executive Director Edward. Clearly that was an oversight. Not a tragedy, just an oversight. The oversight did not sit well with Edward who was having a small-minded moment over the omission.

Unfortunately, Edward was having his small-minded moment while he was sitting directly in front of his computer keyboard.

Uh oh. Don't do it, Ed! Whoops, too late.

Oh baby! Edward, fully in the throes of self-righteous small mindedness, blistered Cammi in an e-mail message. He was well written, to the point, and in the right. However, no matter how much Edward tried to sound professional he sounded like he was fuming. Because he was. It's true when you're on the phone and it's true on e-mail; people can tell if you are fuming.

So Edward fires this rocket off to Cammi. Cammi is very upset and sends an e-mail apology to Edward. She copies Anthony, the President of the Kieran Center's Board of Directors. Anthony is also the Sherwood family's attorney.

Anthony forwards the message to Cooper Sherwood. Cooper Sherwood is exactly who you think he is. He's *Mr. Sherwood.* For our purposes he is Mr. Whizbang, the person of true power. And for the Kieran Center, he is the cash cow.

Four days after Edward sent his burning e-mail message to Cammi he got it forwarded back to him by from Mr. Sherwood.

"Edward, call me immediately, I'd like to discuss this with you."

Edward realizes his small-minded moment was a serious mistake. He stepped on the Emotional E-Mail land mine, a few people made a few clicks, and now he's getting called on the carpet by the Man.

How'd you like to be Edward dialing Mr. Sherwood's phone number?

Me neither.

Avoiding the Emotional E-Mail Land Mine

Avoiding this land mine is not easy, particularly because emotions are involved. When things get tense at work it is normal to have an emotional response. It is also very normal to want to take action, to do *something* about it.

Many times we feel like our point is just not being understood. People just don't "get" it. If they got it, things would be just great.

A natural way to make yourself understood is to write down your points and get them in the hands of the people who need to get it. So the tendency to jump on e-mail seems pretty well thought out on its surface. And maybe, given some time, a brief message clarifying yourself may be in order. But to send an e-mail message while you are feeling the tension, still feeling emotional, can be incendiary to a career.

Avoiding sending combustible e-mail messages takes self discipline. Sometimes it takes quite a bit. Whenever you feel the urge to fire off a blazing message, you need to show a little character and let yourself cool off before you send it. You are going to want to vent your anger in writing and send it right away, but don't do it.

As I've stated, proudly, I am certainly not immune to the occasional small-minded moment. There have been many times when I've wanted to crush my enemies with an e-mail message designed to unmask them for the chuckle-heads they were. Thankfully, I was able to resist the urge.

Here's a trick that has been a great help to me in making sure I do not step on the Emotional E-Mail land mine. Whenever I feel the burning desire to send a nuclear or even a moderately annoyed e-mail message I simply give in to the feeling. That's my advice, if you are having trouble resisting the urge to pound away at your keyboard, articulating your invective, then I say have at it.

Do not, however, under any circumstances use your e-mail program to do it.

It's as simple as that.

I know most e-mail programs will allow you to make a "draft" of a message but I've heard too many horror stories about using that tactic. It is just too easy to make a mistake by hitting "send" by accident or possibly copying an entire group of people who do not need to see the fruits of your small-minded moment. My advice is to close the e-mail program entirely.

What I do is this. I open my word processing program of choice and I rip into whoever needs it. Oh yeah, feels good, let me tell you I enjoy it. It's cathartic. Then, once I've written what I need to write, I save it under some clever false name on my C Drive and leave it there. Then I employ one of my most valuable anger management rules. It's a sacred rule. The rule is, one night's sleep must pass before I read the document again.

Inevitably, when I read the thing the next day I thank my lucky stars I never sent it. On some occasions I've used the less caustic parts of the narrative as notes for what would later become a much more rational, and usually more effective, message.

I'll end this chapter by saying the only real danger about the Emotional E-Mail land mine is the notion that you are not a candidate to write one. Everyone is a candidate. And if you write one and you think no one will ever know how upset you are, I'm pretty sure you'll be mistaken there too.

Take the extra step and write what you need to write, but then use the distance that time gives you to gain a less emotional and a more mature perspective.

Worth Repeating

❖ The world of business is populated by people who have a very deep passion for what they are trying to accomplish. Once in a while, in the course of getting things done, sometimes tempers flare and "sticks come up."

❖ I have never seen an Emotional E-Mail message do anyone any good.

❖ Whenever you feel the urge to fire off a blazing e-mail message you need to show a little character and let yourself cool off before you send it.

❖ If you are having trouble resisting the urge to pound away at your keyboard, articulating your invective, then I say have at it. Do not, however, under any circumstances use your e-mail program to do it.

❖ Let one night's sleep pass before you read the document again.

Section Three: Regular Mail

When I was a marketing exec I used to get a massive amount of mail each day. Piles of it. Every day. It is an absolute fact, in our building at World Headquarters the mail room used to send one of their guys with a cart of mail up the elevator delivering mail *three times a day*. It was ridiculous.

However, as I have previously stated, the greatest corporate perk is the Administrative Assistant. When I was Mr. Whizbang and had an Administrative Assistant, Doris, one of her daily responsibilities was to gather all my daily mail and open it up. She would then separate the mail into four distinct piles:

Pile #1 – *All overnight or priority mail packages*

The Overnight stack was always a mixed bag. Sometimes overnight packages contain something cool, like concert tickets. Once I got one of those Scooters in a big overnight box. Other times it was either something I'd requested from someone, or something boring that had no business being overnighted anywhere.

Pile #2 – Inter-Office mail envelopes

I don't mind admitting that the Inter-Office envelope stack used to strike fear into my heart. And because Inter-Office envelopes could contain confidential personnel material of a highly sensitive nature, these were the only things that Doris was not allowed to open. If you've been in any sizable company you've seen these envelopes. They have the string on the back that you wind around some button mechanism so the envelope becomes impenetrable to anyone who can't unwind the string.

Inter Office envelopes. Ugly things. They're even evil *looking*. Brown. An awful sad brown with black lines upon which the sender would write his or her department so you *knew* who was sending you the documents. So of course that's the first place you look! I would have a visceral reaction from just knowing who sent me an Inter-Office envelope.

My reactions were these:

Inter-Office envelope from Accounting: "Curses! They probably rejected my expense report owing to lack of documentation. They hate me. They've always hated me."

Inter-Office envelope from Legal: "Must be a copy of some vendor contract I signed. I'm sure this has to be filed someplace. Must forward this to Doris."

Inter-Office envelope from Information Services: "This can wait. From the weight of it I bet it's a usage report off the server. I'll leave it on my desk untouched for the next six months. "

Inter-Office envelope from Human Resources: "Aaaaaah!! I'm as doomed as doomed can be. It's a re-org. It's a lawsuit. Or worse, they want me to conduct a meaningful exchange of ideas among my staff and report my findings back on the enclosed form."

Pile #3 – Things that came in a normal envelope of some sort

I always opened the note-card envelopes first and was usually rewarded with happy tidings from friends and colleagues. I'd then move on to the standard size envelopes. The contents of these were all over the map as you might imagine. Then I'd open the larger envelopes which were usually uneventful.

Pile #4 – Catalogues and Magazines

My favorite! The catalogue-and-magazine stack on my desk would grow and grow until it was time for a road trip. The day before I had to fly someplace I would plow through this stack and stuff my briefcase with all manner of high profile forward-thinking corporate business magazines and a catalogue or two. Then on the plane I'd take a highlighter to it all. Rapture.

Safe to say I used to get quite a bit of mail. I still do actually. And while I do mean it when I say that sending material through the mail is a great way to communicate, I also know there are many land mines to set off in this medium.

CHAPTER 11: Land Mine!

The Unsolicited Overnight

Often times a familiar exchange would occur right before I left for a meeting or even a road trip. I'd be at my desk furiously trying to get myself together and the following conversation would ensue:

Doris: (from her desk) Mart... Martin!

Marty: (distracted and woefully unprepared) I'm on my way! I'm like two seconds from on my way here. You have my tickets? Wait, I have them.

Doris: The mail room just dropped off an overnight package for you.

Now at this point I'd have to stop what I was doing and think "Did I order any cool presents for myself off the Internet lately? No. No presents. Then what could this be? Who is overnighting something to me? No one alerted me to this.

Marty: Who's it from?

Doris: Melvin. Melvin from... WhamTronics.

Now there I am at my desk with steam pouring out of my ears as I'm trying to remember if I've ever talked to Melvin or if I've ever heard of WhamTronics. The last thing I need is to get on a plane or go across town and arrive only to find I should have had Melvin's overnight with me.

Marty: What's in it?

Doris: Looks like a big blue folder and a cover letter.

Marty: (still lost) What's WhamTronics do?

Doris: Um... they um, wait... oh here it is, WhamTronics '...is a world leader in providing CRM solutions that–'

Marty: Put it on the stack. I'll look at it when I get back.

It was always worse when I *wasn't* leaving town or on my way to a meeting. It was always worse when I got the Unsolicited Overnight while I was in my office on a normal day making high level decisions and thinking up bold strategies. See, then I had no "Doris Buffer" and I'd have to go through the pain and suffering of figuring out for myself that it wasn't anything that I'd requested.

The Unsolicited Overnight from a vendor always used to perplex me. And I got them all the time. This is a pretty popular land mine.

I get it: someone wants to cut through that pile on Mr. Whizbang's desk. So he puts his brochure or what have you in an overnight envelope or box because he knows it's almost assuredly going to get some attention. And he's right.

Mr. Whizbang gets the overnight package on his desk and of course stops whatever he or she is doing and opens it up right away.

Mission accomplished, no?

Well, maybe, I guess. Sure Mr. Whizbang opened the mailer and looked at the contents. But he or she only did it because a vendor hood-winked him or her into it. My opinion is that the Unsolicited Overnight plan works on paper, but in execution it always seemed a ham-handed tactic. Strictly amateur.

Think about this: How could somebody make the assumption that their material was important enough to overnight to Mr. Whizbang without ever having spoken to Mr. Whizbang at all? The whole thing smacks of sales trickery.

Since trust is an absolute must for getting along in the business universe, why would one want to start out a relationship by sleight-of-handing Mr. Whizbang in any form or fashion? This is clearly not the first impression we want to make on Mr. Whizbang.

Avoiding the Unsolicited Overnight Land Mine

Before you decide to launch an Overnight at Mr. Whizbang without ever having spoken with him or her, consider this: at the heart of the Unsolicited Overnight land mine is the concept of mutuality. Or rather, the lack thereof. You may feel that what you are sending is important. It's vital. The well-being and continued success of Mr. Whizbang's department or company rests squarely on his adopting whatever ideas your overnight package presents. And that may be absolutely true. But Mr. Whizbang does not feel that way because the two of you have never spoken and therefore could not agree that the information is worth overnighting to him.

DEFINITION
mutual (adjective): a) directed by each toward the other or the others; b) having the same feelings one for the other; c) shared in common

---

Agreement. Mutuality. These must be in place *before* we start loading up the planes with our brochures.

Of course the easy answer is to get Mr. Whizbang on the phone and engage him or her in a conversation that will lead logically to you sending on the necessary information.

That is easier said than done.

If you're trying to contact a Mr. Whizbang who is extremely hard to get, the chances are he or she is either:

    A. Very skilled at avoiding vendors, salespeople and job applicants and as such ought to be pushed out a second story window into a row of unpleasant shrubs, or

    B. He or she truly is a Whizbang and if we ever do get to him or her we can move the process along.

In the case of someone who is difficult to get, I certainly hope that you have many more experiences chasing the latter than the former. I have had all too much experience in my professional life chasing folks who I thought were people of true power, only to find they were just suits taking up space on the organizational chart.

Let's say you are having little success in generating a dialogue of any kind with a true Mr. Whizbang. And let's say that Mr. Whizbang is within moderate driving distance.

My advice is this: Take whatever you were going to Overnight to Mr. Whizbang and put it in a normal envelope. Handwrite Mr. Whizbang's name on the front of the envelope and drive it over to his or her office.

When you get to the front desk do NOT ask to see Mr. Whizbang. Ask to see Mr. Whizbang's assistant. If you are very lucky you will be asked to sit down and wait. If your luck holds out, Mr. Whizbang's assistant will eventually appear and this will be your opportunity to hand him or her the package and to establish some rapport with him or her.

Even if you get shut down by the receptionist with an efficient "Oh you can just leave it with me and I'll see Mr. Whizbang gets this" you are still better off than if you had just Overnighted the material to him or her. I've had a fair amount of success with the dropping-it-off method. It shows a bit of effort and lacks the slight of hand of an Unsolicited Overnight. Something without a post mark of any kind is going to stick out in Mr. Whizbang's desk. Also, it implies, correctly, that someone (you) took the time and effort out of his or her day to make a personal visit. This may resonate with Mr. Whizbang.

Because of his lofty position on the corporate totem pole, Spike got even more mail than I did. If I were truly lucky, I'd be in Spike's office when his assistant, Wanda, would walk in with an Unsolicited Overnight package for Spike. Invariably it would be something cute like a yo-yo, a pen, a tool kit, a baseball cap, a notebook, a coffee mug, or some other wildly creative promo item designed to make Spike stop his day and pine away for that company's products.

> Spike: Gee, I wish they'd call me. I have no idea who they are or what they do, but that is one *heck* of a yoyo.

It was my experience that Spike never did have that reaction.

More often, Spike would open the package, hold up the item and say to me "Want it?" Usually I'd say "Nope" and he'd toss it. He was heartless that way.

Me, I always felt a little guilty when someone would send me an unsolicited promo item. If it was a particularly attractive or useful item I always hoped it was from a company with whom I could genuinely do business. But, unfortunately, most times it was from a company that had no idea what I was trying to accomplish because they never took the time and effort to find out.

As I mentioned earlier, late in the year 2000 some nice Dot Com company actually overnighted to me one of those cool scooters that were so popular at the time. I was very pleased. In fact, I gave it to my six-year old son who was even more pleased that I was.

The scooter came with no cover letter. Just the scooter. I assumed that this was an oversight and that some sales person would soon call and ask me "So, Mart, you get the scooter I sent?" But no call ever came. I did a little checking and found out this Dot Com company was probably not a tight fit for what I was doing in my department. If anyone had called, or even sent an e-mail message, I may have been able to save him the trouble. And the postage.

The Unsolicited Overnight is a land mine in sheep's clothing. It looks like a good idea but in the end it sends a bad message to Mr. Whizbang. It is a very low percentage play. The chances of Mr. Whizbang throwing aside whatever you decided was important enough to use an overnight service to mail to him or her is extremely high. Why would being tossed aside be your choice of a first impression?

Let's pretend you had an aunt and uncle who would, without invitation, drop by your family's house on a random weeknight, bringing with them three or four carousels of vacation slides and a projector. While you have the picture of your aunt and uncle standing in your foyer smiling sanctimoniously, imagine how your parents felt. Interrupted. Inconvenienced. And probably entirely uninterested. Now, your parents *have to* tolerate your aunt and uncle's visit and slide show with a smile, some polite ooh's and aah's, and perhaps a coffee. What they'd like to do is toss the slides and the projector in the garbage and ask your aunt and uncle to beat it.

Mr. Whizbang does not have to tolerate anything and he or she will more than likely do to you and your Unsolicited Overnight what your parents wish they could do to your aunt, your uncle, the slides, and the projector.

Worth Repeating

❖ Mr. Whizbang only looked at your Unsolicited Overnight because he or she was hood-winked into it.

❖ The Unsolicited Overnight plan works on paper but in execution it is a ham-handed tactic. Strictly amateur.

❖ Trust is an absolute must for getting along in the business universe. Why start out a relationship by sleight-of-handing Mr. Whizbang in any form or fashion?

❖ Agreement. Mutuality. These must be in place *before* we start loading up the planes with our brochures.

❖ Whenever possible, take whatever you were going to overnight to Mr. Whizbang and put it in a normal envelope. Handwrite Mr. Whizbang's name on the front of the envelope and drive it over to his or her office.

CHAPTER 12: Land Mine!

The Sanitary Mailer

At my desk back at World Headquarters I used to get as much mass mail as I did mail from individual people.

When anyone gets anything in the mail that they do not instantly recognize there are a few things they try to find, Mr. Whizbang included. People are looking for an indication of *connection* with another person. In these days of information overload, the human touch is increasingly rare.

The Sanitary Mailer land mine is triggered any time someone sends something to Mr. Whizbang through the mail and the material has never been touched by human hands except to stuff it into the envelope.

No, your signature on the cover letter does not count.

When Mr. Whizbang opens a letter or a package of some kind a few thoughts run through his or her head:

◆ Who sent this?
◆ What is it?
◆ Why did they send it?
◆ Is there something specific to which I ought to be paying attention?
◆ Is this some sort of mass mailing?
◆ Is this thing, at this very moment, wasting my time?

If Mr. Whizbang ever gets to that last question, the answer is probably yes, it is a waste of time.

The key is to use any method you can to get Mr. Whizbang the answers to these questions as soon as possible. A completely Sanitary Mailer, without any sign of human hands being laid upon it, makes it tough for the recipient to navigate to the information most pertinent to his or her situation. Even the most patient recipient (and again, I can assure you "patience" is probably not one of Mr. Whizbang's virtues) will probably dread wading through your information.

Mr. Whizbang will not wade through it. He or she will toss it.

My boss Spike was very influential. Spike signed the contracts to buy multimillion dollar pieces of equipment, he negotiated deals to buy millions of dollars of advertising, and he had the decision-making power over 350 jobs in the sales force and marketing team.

Get to Spike and you had a shot to impress Spike. Impress Spike and you could get somewhere with our company. The distance from Spike's desk to his trash can was extremely short. Some stuff stayed on the desk. The majority got tossed.

Things that stayed on Spike's Desk
- ◆ Stuff he'd requested
- ◆ Stuff from people he knew
- ◆ Stuff from people to whom he'd previously spoken
- ◆ Stuff from companies he recognized

Anything that did not fit into one of those categories quickly was in grave danger of being pitched. The average piece of mail got about six seconds of eye-ball time with Spike. He just did not have the time to read through all the material he got sent to him.

The key to staying on both Spike's and Mr. Whizbang's desk is to make that human connection with him or her as quickly as possible. Even if Mr. Whizbang *requested* the information it is not a very good practice to just jam it in an envelope and send it off.

Making that human connection and avoiding stepping on the Sanitary Mailer land mine in your regular mail correspondence is actually pretty easy but it has been my experience that very few people take the time to do it. Again, this is good news for you in your efforts to set yourself apart and ahead of the crowd.

Avoiding the Sanitary Mailer Land Mine

Making the human connection is everything. Let me use an example or two to illustrate my point.

Did you ever get something in the mail that *looked*, at first glance, like someone had actually written you a note on the envelope or in the margin of the letter, brochure, catalogue, whatever? But then when you looked closely it was clear that this was a pre-printed note. No one actually wrote that note. But think, why did they take the time to print it that way?

While you ponder, think about this one:

Have you ever received mail that *looked* like it had a Post-it® Note stuck on it with a handwritten note but when you examined it you saw that this was just part of the mass mail? No one actually stuck that Post-it® Note on there and no actual live human being wrote you a nice note on it. So why put it there?

Think. Why do mass mailers do these things? What is the point of marking up a perfectly nice piece of mass mail with faux handwritten notes? Easy, they know, those naughty mass mailing people, they *know* the recipient will look twice at the piece if he or she thought an actual person touched it and wrote a note.

The tactics I mention above are tricks, deceptions, clever ruses designed to grab your attention. That's the game with mass mail. Mass mailers will do anything to get your attention even if it involves tactics that are designed specifically to fool you. The reason they do these things is because they *work*. These tactics tap into the involuntary response most people have when they see something in the mail that they think another person has sent to them specifically.

So, am I suggesting that you adopt the tactics of the mass-mailers and try to fake Mr. Whizbang into looking at your mail piece?

No. Certainly not. Making the human connection is everything. *Faking* the human connection is underhanded.

So how do you *make* the human connection with your mail pieces to Mr. Whizbang? I have some suggestions that should be very easy to implement.

Get your checkbook out. You are going to need supplies.

The Sharpie® Marker

Look at your desk. Survey the landscape of your workspace. If you do not find a Sharpie® marker, go out and buy a three-pack instantly. The Sharpie® marker, a gift to the business world from the good people at Sanford, is one of your best friends in your effort to make the human connection. My advice is to buy the super-versatile Sharpie® Twin Tip. As its name implies, it has two tips, one thick, one thin. Genius. Beyond genius. When you get to the exit for genius, keep going because the Twin Tip is beyond genius. I kid you not.

Now, having acquired a few Sharpies, you can begin to make the human connection by marking up anything you send to Mr. Whizbang. And I mean anything. Except formal documents like contracts, nothing should leave your desk without being marked up in some form. You do not have to write a lengthy note. All you really have to do is make an obvious mark.

I was consulting with a multi media company who had great looking brochures that complimented their excellent product lines. During the course of a networking event, one of the company's partners, Bruce, met the Product Manager of a brand new pharmaceutical company. Through their conversation it became clear that the Product Manager, Roy, would benefit greatly from a CD-ROM created to educate sales reps on the merits of the company's new medication.

Roy: So does your company write the training material and then send the training modules out to get pressed on CD's?

Bruce: Actually no. We would take your existing materials, format them for production on CD-ROM, and then produce the CD's in-house.

Roy: Good, because we already have the material written but we need someone to turn it into a CD deliverable for our sales team.

Bruce: We'd love to do it. Do you have a card?

Roy: Sure, here you go. Can you send me something I can show to my Director of Training?

Bruce: Absolutely. Here's my card. If you get a chance, take a look at our Web site. I'll put something in the mail tomorrow and follow up with you toward the end of the week.

Roy: Great. Nice to meet you. I'm going to go eat the rest of those stuffed mushrooms before some-one else gloms them.

Bruce: Go for it. Nice to meet you too.

Bruce gets in the next day and he's all set to slam a brochure with a cover letter into a nice clean envelope and get it mailed out as promised.

> *Mail nothing that you have not personally marked up in some form or fashion.*
> --M. Clarke

But he stops. And he remembers that NOTHING must leave his desk without his handwriting on it. So he finds a Sharpie (any pen will do, I just happen to be a Sharpie® zealot) and he opens the brochure.

His brochure, like almost all others, is a well-thought out summary of his company's product lines. *Lines.* As in plural. His company provided many more services than just the CD-ROM production he discussed with Roy.

Bruce uncaps his marker and draws a circle around the CD-ROM production section of the brochure and he writes a small note: "Roy, here is the information you need. Talk with you soon!" And he sends the marked up brochure out. Simple.

When Roy gets this brochure in the mail, he'll notice that someone has laid personal hands on it. He'll see imme-diately what it's about, and he'll remember his conversation with Bruce.

Roy: Oh yeah, this is the guy I met at that thing the other night. Excellent. I need to show this to...

The human connection is made. You have to mark up everything you send. Do not be afraid to draw circles, arrows, and the like with a note that says, "Mr. Whizbang, here's what you need to see."

The residual effects are that Mr. Whizbang will appreciate your getting to your point quickly and it will remind him or her that he or she has previously spoken with you.

The Yellow Highlighter

I specify yellow only as a personal preference. Besides yellow, highlighters these days come in blue, pink, orange, green, and I'm sure they are staying up nights coming out with more as we speak.

Just as Sharpie® markers work well on brochures, highlighters work well on letters. Whenever I've finished a letter to someone I always like to highlight a word or a phrase that I definitely want the recipient to see. Then I write a little note in pen beside it like "Ben, here's the date for our meeting."

Actually, highlighters are great for any correspondence where a lot of text appears in one place. A favorite tactic of mine continues to be clipping magazine articles out of whatever magazine I happen to be reading and then highlighting a few words or sentences that might mean something to a prospect or a customer. I can be almost entirely assured that if the recipient opens the mail piece their eyes will be drawn quickly to what I have highlighted for them.

I don't presume to make the recipient read the entire article. If they want to they will. I just want to draw their attention to a specific part which will give me a reason to follow up with a phone call later.

The key is, if I've highlighted it and written a small note, the recipient will know that it has been touched by human hands.

The Post-it® Note

It does not matter what color Post-it® Note gets used in business correspondence. Buy a rainbow colored cube of them and use any color you like.

But use them.

The Post-it® Note is a critical human connection device. I mean real Post-it® Notes upon which you actually write things, not the ersatz Post-it® Notes with pre-printed messages favored by the mass mailers. Oh, how they defile Art Fry and his invention! Did Art invent the Post-it® Note so it could be used by the mass-mailers in an effort to fool their audience? I should say not.

If you do not feel comfortable writing on or marking up a particular mail piece (a contract, a proposal, a cover letter...) you can always use a Post-it® Note to give you a small but noticeable area in which to write a short note.

In general, it is acceptable to affix a Post-it® Note to anything. Let's say I decide to send an entire magazine to Mr. Whizbang. If I do, I am sure to place a Post-it® Note on the article I want Mr. Whizbang to read. I would of course leave a bit of it hanging out over the edge. On this portion of the note I would write Mr. Whizbang's name. This is an instant visual alert that says "Look here. Now! This information is specifically for you."

DEFINITION
specific (adjective): a) restricted to a particular individual, situation, relation, or effect; b) free from ambiguity

---

Have you ever received anything in the mail that had a Post-it® Note marking a page and *not* turned to that page instantly?

Neither will Mr. Whizbang. Now go one step further and highlight a sentence or a phrase in the body of the article and then write a short note next to it.

A word about writing notes on things. First off, a handwritten *something* is always going to get more attention than a typed *anything*. And since brochures, proposals, and resumes are typed entities, we should take every opportunity to handwrite something on them to humanize the experience for the recipient.

The sweetest sound to any human being is the sound of their own name. Whenever possible, use the recipient's name at the start of the note. It may sound trivial but if there is one single thing for which your eyes, my eyes, and Mr. Whizbang's eyes are trained to scan, it is our own name. If it's typed we notice it. If someone has *handwritten* our name, we are absolutely rivetted by it. If you want to make that human connection, find a reason to mark up the mailer and write the recipient's name.

By the way, I estimate the supplies needed to upgrade your mail correspondence and avoid the Sanitary Mailer land mine will cost you in the neighborhood of $17.00. My guess is that most professionals spend more than that on one trip to the dry cleaner. In any event, it is a small investment that can certainly pay off by getting Mr. Whizbang's attention.

Worth Repeating

❖ When opening his or her mail Mr. Whizbang is looking for an indication of a *connection* with another person. In these days of mass mail and general information overload, the human touch is increasingly rare.

❖ A completely Sanitary Mailer, without any sign of human hands being laid upon it makes it tough for the recipient to navigate to the information most pertinent to his or her situation.

❖ The key to staying on Mr. Whizbang's desk is to make that human connection with him or her as quickly as possible.

❖ Get a few Sharpie® markers and let nothing leave your desk without you marking something on it.

❖ Use yellow highlighters.

❖ Post-it® Notes are great for making notes on contracts or anything upon which a large amount of text appears.

❖ When making notes on a mailer use Mr. Whizbang's name if at all possible.

CHAPTER 13: Land Mine!

The Metric Ton Mailer

The guys down in the mail room must have hated me. Not only did I get an amazing amount of mail, but I also got many mail pieces of staggering size and heft. I used to get giant envelopes jam-packed with information. Binders, notebooks, presentations, collections of brochures, giant brochures that had *other* brochures inside them, the list went on and on.

Even when I'd actually requested information, it seemed that I triggered the "send him everything!" response. I do not know why that was. I assure you I never once stopped my entire day to pore over someone else's product information. Typically I'd sift through it quickly, trying to find the specific information I needed.

I remember very well a time when my boss Spike made a rare cameo appearance in my office. Typically I was summoned upstairs to Spike's office. So when he appeared on the 8th floor it was usually something pretty important.

Spike: Who were you on the phone with?

Marty: When?

Spike: Just now.

Marty: Just now? Um that was, I was on with Service
Implementation. We have...

149

Spike: I've been trying to get you for twenty minutes. Get your notebook out.

"Get your notebook out" was boss talk for "I'm about to assign you a task and it would be very bad if you did not get it done quickly and perfectly."

Marty: (notebook out, pen in hand) Ok, go.

Spike: I want someone on your team to do the research on buying a 20-foot trade show booth. Custom made. We want whoever it is to handle design, construction, shipping and storage. It's got to be computer ready and it needs mounts for two plasma screens.

Marty: (not looking up) Got it.

Spike: I want a summary page on my desk by Tuesday and if you can, some sample pictures.

Marty: Got it. What else?

Spike: Nothing. Just jump on it. This thing has to be approved, built, and standing tall at the Mega-Com show.

Marty: MegaCom as in the MegaCom show in two months?

Spike: That's the one.

Marty: Nice lead time, Chief.

Spike: Don't get mouthy. Just get it done.

Marty: We're on it.

I assigned this to a very reliable member of my team, Jennifer. I gave Jennifer the rundown, and off we went. After a little Internet research I think she called five companies who did the high level custom work we needed.

Then the avalanche came. These companies started sending giant envelopes of information. All we wanted was some sample pictures and maybe some price ranges. But we got metric tons of mail. It was ridiculous. Then apparently somebody somewhere leaked it that we were in the market for a custom trade show booth and we started getting huge mailers from companies we didn't even know. Actually, I didn't mind that part of it. You never know when you're going to stumble over a great vendor. But the information they sent made it very hard to figure that out. It just kept piling up. Eventually anyone who entered this poor Jennifer's cube had to step around the "Trade Show stuff."

We didn't even know where to begin and we were under the gun to get this figured out. So we naturally gravitated to the companies who sent simple, to the point mailers that quickly and simply provided the information we wanted.

We eventually waded through all of it, but it got to the point that we'd cringe when we had to open a huge box from some company because we knew that while the information we needed was probably in there, it was a chore to sift through everything else to find it.

From my point of view, The Metric Ton Mailer is a land mine born out of sheer laziness. Instead of picking out the information Mr. Whizbang wants, people who fall victim to the Metric Ton Mailer send him or her everything they have. Then it's up to Mr. Whizbang to search for what he or she needs.

When Mr. Whizbang says "Send me some information" he or she means "some" information. Moreover, when Mr. Whizbang says "some information" he or she means the information that means something to him or her specifically and not much else.

Avoiding the Metric Ton Mailer Land Mine

Your ears are your best friends in avoiding this land mine. We could spend a lot of time rehashing the finer points of listening skills. I'm not going to go into that right now. You have ears, use them.

Sometimes, however, Mr. Whizbang will be a little vague. When that happens, here's a question that will help you help Mr. Whizbang bring into clearer definition what information of yours will make the most sense for him or her. Any time Mr. Whizbang asks you to "Send some information" you may want to reply with:

"Absolutely. Is there anything specific I should include?"

This will give Mr. Whizbang the opportunity to be specific. Don't worry, there will be time to cross sell, up sell, and otherwise load up Mr. Whizbang later. For now, give the people what they want. You can do this by asking that question.

Very rarely will Mr. Whizbang reply with a glib "Nope. Send me everything you have!" This is because Mr. Whizbang does not want everything you have. My experience has been that Mr. Whizbang usually replies with something pretty definite. I've used the "is there anything specific" question for years.

1992 – Selling Telecommunications

Mr. Whizbang the Owner: Yeah, go ahead and send me some information.

Marty: Absolutely. Is there anything specific I should include?

Mr. Whizbang: Not really. Well, actually, make sure you include a map of your data network.

1998 – Trying to get a feature article written about our company

Mr. Whizbang the Business Editor: Yeah, go ahead and send me some information.

Marty: Absolutely. Is there anything specific I should include?

Mr. Whizbang: If you have a one-pager with your executive bios on it I usually like to start there.

2002 – Positioning a Training Program

Mr. Whizbang the Director of Corporate Education: Yeah, go ahead and send me some information.

Marty: Absolutely. Is there anything specific I should include?

Mr. Whizbang: Um, include something that shows your experience in developing coursework specifically for sales managers.

Almost every time I asked this question, Mr. Whizbang gave me a very clear hint for as to what he or she wanted to accomplish with the information. I believe the same will prove true for you. The "is there anything specific" question will give you all the information you need to avoid triggering the Metric Ton Mailer land mine. You can reduce the stacks of information you were about to send. Knowing this, if you still feel compelled to empty the marketing closet into an oversized envelope and send it along, punishing letter carriers and contributing to the mailroom's mounting hatred of unnecessary information, please put the "something specific" information someplace obvious so Mr. Whizbang can get to it quickly.

One of the biggest "Will you please go away" lines in the business world is "Send me some information." Some folks are pretty non-confrontational and instead of declining you politely they'll ask you to send information and then pray you never follow up and if you do, they may dodge you.

For the record, I have nothing but contempt for these people and wish them a lifetime of misery.

If you are on the phone with Mr. Whizbang and he or she hits you with "Go ahead and send some information." and you bat the ball back over the net with "Absolutely. Is there anything specific I should include?" and then Mr. Whizbang fumbles around and gives you only half an answer, or an answer that does not make much sense (you watch, it'll happen), then it is my suggestion that one or more of the following is true:

Mr. Whizbang:

◆ Was only half listening to you anyway

◆ Has no intention of looking at your material

◆ Is not really Mr. Whizbang and hasn't a clue
    or a care as to how your offering will impact
    the company

If any of these scenarios fits, send something anyway. You never know. But I wouldn't be counting on an immediate call back and I wouldn't waste a lot of valuable time chasing this person.

Worth Repeating

❖ Mr. Whizbang will naturally gravitate to the companies and people who send simple, to-the-point mailers that quickly provide the information he or she wants.

❖ When Mr. Whizbang says "some information" he or she means the information that means something to him or her specifically, and not much else.

❖ Ask Mr. Whizbang the question "Is there anything specific I should include?" And then use your ears.

Section Four:
Face to Face

Five minutes in front of the right audience can be worth more than a year behind your desk.
--Granville Toogood, The Articulate Executive

Granville is right. The face-to-face meeting is huge. If you want to talk about a make or break situation, many times the face-to-face meeting is it. Job interviews or sales calls, it makes no never mind, the face-to-face is usually when we find out who wins and who loses.

Here are two stories to illustrate:

Story #1 Marty and the Smell Test

Recently, my buddy Dave brought me into a consulting contract to write a very specific training program for a company in South Carolina. A fee was agreed upon and I was thrilled to get going on the project. I produced the course work, the workbooks, and the presentation.

In the fullness of time I sent the drafts to Dave so that he could present them to the company executives. They wanted, of course, to review the material I'd be presenting to their Sales Managers. I thought the materials turned out very well but I was, as I always am, interested to know the opinion of the folks who were buying my programs.

Dave returned from that meeting and the following conversation ensued:

Marty: What did they think?

Dave: We're fine. They want us to do it in sixty days. They're bringing all their managers in to headquarters for two days. We're on in the afternoon of day one.

Marty: Excellent! I'm so psyched. Think I'll even shine my shoes.

Dave: Better shine 'em tonight.

Marty: Why?

Dave: They want to meet you.

Marty: The execs?

Dave: Yep. Don't get uptight. It's just a smell test.

Marty: Smell test.

Dave: Yeah. Look, for the money they're investing they want to meet you face-to-face. Give you the smell test.

Marty: So, if I understand this correctly, to show up and smell bad would be a poorly thought out plan.

Dave: Mart, don't be difficult. You know the drill. Get your calendar out and let's see when you can get to South Carolina.

So I gladly made the trip down to South Carolina. I wore a nice suit, smelled great, spoke in full sentences and all was well. The point was, they wanted the face-to-face meeting before they went ahead with the deal.

Story #2 Ted and the Seven-Figure Gift

A few years ago I got a call from a great guy named Ted. Ted was, and continues to be, a great mentor of mine and a very influential man in general. But try as he might he was having no luck prizing out of our company a considerable sum of money he wanted donated to an extremely worthy charity.

Ted knew I was way too low on the totem pole to help him directly but he called and asked me if I could tell him how to get in front of the Chairman.

I told him that pretty much no one got in front of the Chairman and his best bet was to try the General Counsel, Jean Paul. Jean Paul was also the Chairman's personal lawyer. That was about the best I could do for Ted.

Ted got a face-to-face with Jean Paul. Jean Paul surfaced the idea of the donation to the Chairman. It turns out the Chairman enjoyed a much deserved reputation for making these types of contributions, especially when they benefited the local area, which this donation would.

A few more meetings took place over the next few weeks. Long story short, Ted eventually got precisely the amount of money he requested. It was a significant sum of money. Though I'm sure many phone calls were made in the course of this venture, it is my belief that a gift of this size would not have been given if communication took place solely over the phone.

In both cases the deal hinged on a face-to-face meeting.

I've spent the last eleven or twelve years in an incalculable number of face-to-face situations. I've either been fighting to get into somebody's office to get face-to-face with them or having someone fighting to get into mine to get face-to-face with me. Later in my career, I was responsible for being the voice of my superiors when I traveled out in the sales territories. It was incumbent upon me in that role to be on the road, making presentations in front of sales people, in front of operations people, and in front of customers. During that time I also accompanied countless sales professionals on appointments up and down the East Coast, and sometimes across the country.

I have had a ringside seat to watch the Face to Face land mines going off and to trigger a few myself. It's a chancy little drama, the face-to-face meeting. A lot can go wrong on a job interview, a sales call, or any other in-person meeting of any magnitude. The key is to minimize the chances that catastrophe will strike by understanding the land mines that are littering the face-to-face meeting and taking the necessary steps to avoid them. Since the face-to-face meeting is so critical, avoiding these land mines can be one of the absolute *best* ways to set yourself apart.

CHAPTER 14: Land Mine!

Dress Code

Ask a product manager at Procter & Gamble, or Hewlett-Packard, or any business you like if packaging is important to the success of their brand and after they stop hyperventilating they'll tell you "yes." America buys the box. And no doubt about it. And your dress code is a critical part of your personal packaging.

"But wait Mart, these are the days of 'business casual.' This is the new economy. We don't need that suit and tie jazz anymore. That mentality is over with. Right?"

Um, no, it isn't. I don't care what days these are or what economy this is. If you want to make a good impression during the face-to-face meeting, dress the part. And when in doubt, over-dress a bit.

Any time I go to meet a client or a potential client, I wear a tie. If only to impart a tacit sign of respect. If the client tells me that the next time we meet they'd prefer I dress casually, then I do. But not until they tell me. If you want to be taken seriously, my advice is to over dress just a bit.

I used to work with this guy to whom I will refer as the Glass Man. The Glass Man was a rare gem of an employee for quite a few reasons. One of his gifts was his ability in front of an audience. He transmitted credibility with every word out of his mouth. This was simply because he was

160

without peer in his knowledge of his particular discipline. In an effort to put the Company's best foot forward I tried to keep The Glass Man in front of as many of our sales people and customers as possible. While he was working on my team he used to have to fly quite a bit. He explained the reasons for proper aviator dress code this way:

> The Glass Man: Mart, you know I'm a good flier. Flying doesn't bother me. Rain. Turbulence. Whatever. I never worry. Wanna know why?

> Marty: Lay it on me.

> The Glass Man: When I walk onto a plane I always sneak a look left into the cockpit. Every time. I always look into the cockpit. And every time I do I see one or two people sitting there in that cramped space going over charts and flipping switches. But I don't care what they're doing. I care what they're *wearing*.

> Marty: Pilot stuff.

> The Glass Man: You bet they are. They always wear the nice white shirts with epaulets on their shoulders and maybe a blue pilot's cap. And this is just as it should be.

> Marty: That's what pilots look like.

> The Glass Man: That's my point! Does that make them fly better? No. But let me tell you this, if I'm ever getting on a plane and I see two people sitting there in the cockpit and they're wearing khaki's and golf shirts, I'm turning around and running my little legs back up the jetway fast like you read about. No way I'm getting on that plane.

> Marty: Me neither.

The Glass Man: Of course not. And you could tell me these were the two most reliable and gifted pilots in the history of recorded flight and I'd still tell you no way.

The Glass Man has a point. Pilots look the part for a reason. So do doctors, law enforcement personnel, lab scientists and business people. What they wear sends a message to their audience. They know that anyone who meets you or even sees you is going to have some sort of visceral response to the way you physically present yourself. Leaving nothing to chance, you want to make sure this response is positive.

I interviewed many job applicants during my tenure in Corporate Headquarters and I will tell you that for better or worse, how the candidate presented him- or herself counted. It just did.

For example, I interviewed a young lady once for a mid-level marketing job. We met in a coffee shop. I got there early and grabbed a seat. I'd only talked with her on the phone so I had no idea what she looked like. As I sat reading the paper I kept looking up as people entered the store.

One of the times I looked up I saw a young lady with short black hair, wearing a yellow sundress and sandals. I immediately went back to my paper. This obviously was not a job applicant.

Poorly-Dressed Girl: Are you Marty Clarke?

Marty: (initially stunned but recovering quickly) Yes! You must be Liz. Sit down, sit down.

Liz: Thanks.

That interview did not start off well for Liz, the poorly-dressed girl. I did not hire her for several reasons, but the point is that she had unwittingly set herself up with an obstacle before she even started. Would it have been too terribly difficult to throw on a suit or something a bit more professional for a job interview? She was either lazy or just plain ignorant. Either way, she had stepped on the Dress Code land mine and that in and of itself didn't ruin her chances, but it clearly didn't help.

Avoiding the Dress Code Land Mine

The short answer is: Dress the Part. If you need help there are many texts on proper business attire to which you can refer. I will offer this: Shoes count. I cannot say why, nor do I think anyone knows why, but shoes count. Beyond that, if you want to be treated like a pro, dress like a pro.

I remember one particular Dress Code situation vividly. This was a situation when I avoided triggering the Dress Code land mine in a very large way.

It was spring and I was working in the marketing department. I got a call from Spike. But I did not know it was from Spike. The screen on my phone was blinking the President's name at me. Holy schmoly, Rex is calling me. Even though Rex was, and is, a great guy who always treated me like gold, I was still all aflutter. He was the President after all. He was my boss's boss. The following conversation ensued:

Marty: Yes sir.

Spike: Hey, it's Spike.

Marty: You're in Rex's office?

Spike: Nothing gets by you. Get on up here.

Marty: To Rex's office.

Spike: No, to the Break Room. I want you to guard the Snapple Machine.

Marty: Nice. What's going on?

Spike: By the time I explain it you could be here.

Marty: On my way.

I grabbed my notebook and it was exactly then that I realized what I was wearing. It was a day when I wasn't required to see customers and on those days Spike allowed us to dress casually.

I was wearing loafers, no socks, pale yellow pants with triple pleats and baby cuffs, and a pale green madras shirt. My own staff was mortified at my attire and now I was going up to the ninth floor. Maybe Spike wouldn't notice.

In Rex's giant corner office I found Rex on the phone. He was visibly upset, and Spike was sitting across the desk from him pointing at the empty chair next to him. I sat down and waited.

Rex: (into the phone and fortunately paying no attention to me) Trunk side! Trunk side! The problem's on the trunk side. If you have a trunk side issue why in the world are you testing the line side? Of course the line side's gonna test clean...

Spike: (in a low voice to me) Nice pants.

Marty: (in an equally low voice) Leave me alone. What's this about?

Spike: Your wife see you like that? She let you leave the house like that?

Marty: You wish you had these pants.

Rex: (still on the phone) Did you call Seaside yet? Get John Seaside on the phone. If Seaside says the problem's on the line side, then I'll believe it.

Spike: Shirt's lovely too. You look like second prize at an Easter Egg Hunt.

Marty: You're the wind beneath my wings.

Rex: (to Spike, holding the phone away from his ear) …I got five guys working on the problem I got nobody working on the solution. Everyone is standing around telling me how it can't happen when I know it can. I built the first one we installed. Hiya Mart.

Marty: Rex.

Rex: Spike, why's he here?

Spike: He's going to take care of that…

Rex: Oh yeah. Here. Mart. Here's the customer file for Mango Travel. They just called and cancelled their service. It's all in the file. You get over there right away; they're just up on Lynne Road. You get up there and you make sure we keep them as a customer. You do what you gotta do, but if I see them on the disconnect list anytime in the next week or so I'm gonna be asking you why. Got it?

Marty: (standing) I'm all over it.

Rex: Mart, we are not going to lose a five year customer over a two day problem.

Marty: (leaving) On it.

Rex: My man.

Spike: Good luck, sweetheart.

On the one hand, I was very pleased to get the assignment. They wouldn't have sent me if they didn't trust I could get the job done. So I was pretty happy about that.

On the other hand I was about to visit, uninvited, a customer that had already called and cancelled their service.

Apparently they were upset that we knocked them out of service for two days. This was going to be an inhospitable, possibly very hostile place as far as my presence was concerned.

So at this point I had a choice:

1. Walk in there as I was, dressed in my Spring Bouquet outfit; or
2. Go home, jump into a suit and tie and then visit Mango Travel.

And this illustrates my point exactly. Who in their right mind would arrive at the offices of a valued customer dressed casually? No one. Why not? Because in that situation and in many many others you want to be taken seriously: you want to make a solid, professional impression on your audience immediately.

So dress the part. Job interview, sales call, whatever. If it's face-to-face, dressing up is better than dressing down.

By the way, the Mango Travel story has a very happy ending.

I did go home and jump into my darkest blue suit, a crisp white shirt, and a red "I'll Be In Charge Now" tie, and wing tips. I looked like I worked for the Secret Service. Perfect.

I walked into Mango Travel and presented myself to Betty who not only owned the place but had borne the brunt of our service issue.

Once I was in her office Betty vented. Then she took a breath. Then she vented again. Eventually she ran out of steam. They all do, you know. And that's pretty much all she wanted to do. She wanted to be heard by someone in authority. I assured her that the President had personally requested I visit her. I also apologized on behalf of the company. It's amazing what that can do to an irate customer. A simple apology is an excellent calming agent. I advised her that I had the authority to make whatever amends she thought was fair in order to keep her as a customer. After we agreed on two free months of service I drove back to headquarters.

When I went back up to the ninth floor to return the file, Spike came out of his office and fell in step with me as I walked down the hall.

Spike: They staying?

Marty: Yep.

Spike: (smiling) That suit looks terrible by the way.

Marty: It's my best one.

Spike: Nice job, Mart.

Marty: Thanks.

Worth Repeating

❖ What you wear sends a message to your audience.

❖ If you want to be treated like a Pro, dress like a Pro.

❖ Shoes count.

❖ Anyone who meets you or even sees you is going to have some sort of visceral response to the way you physically present yourself. Leaving nothing to chance, you want to make sure this response is positive.

❖ In all professional situations you want to be taken seriously, you want to make a solid, professional impression on your audience immediately. In this regard, your dress is either working for you or against you.

CHAPTER 15: Land Mine!

Lack of Leadership

This one used to drive me bats both when I was going on calls with my reps as well as later, when I was on the other side of the desk. But then again, I stepped on this land mine a few times myself when I was a sales person.

As a Sales Manager it would not be uncommon for me to go on several appointments with various reps in a single day. I'd be in the passenger seat of some rep's nice car, parked in a visitor's spot in front of an office building. I would invariably turn to the rep before we got out of the car and say

"Ok, give me an idea of what's going to go on in this meeting."

The answer I usually got back would fall into two distinct categories

    1. "Not a clue, Mart!" or,

    2. "Here's the plan."

It would have saved me a lot of time and heartache if the reps whose answers eventually fell into the first category would have just responded in those exact words. But instead it went more like this:

> Marty: Ok Barry, give me an idea of what's going to go on in this meeting.

Barry: Well, I called this guy for about like a month. Remember?

Marty: Vividly.

Barry: Yeah, so I was calling and calling and finally I got through to Mr. Whizbang's admin and she told me he usually gets in around 7:45 in the morning.

Marty: Yes, I remember you immediately put this company on your 60-day forecast after having that conversation with her.

Barry: Right. These guys spend a ton.

Marty: So what's going to go on once we get in there?

Barry: Um, well, we'll be meeting with him and maybe his accounting guy. We should be able to see what they're spending and then come back with a proposal.

At this point the conversation would have put me in mortal fear of a spontaneous nosebleed. Why hadn't Barry just said "No clue, Mart! I got the appointment didn't I? Wahoooo!"

Had Barry just said that, which was the absolute truth, I would have been fine with it. Unfortunately, Barry was jumping up and down on the Lack of Leadership land mine and he had no idea he was doing it.

Now, as an aside, let me just say that as the Sales Manager in this situation I had a choice. I could rescue Barry from his own Lack of Leadership and, once we got into the meeting, *I* could lead the meeting for him. And in that case I would be acting as a surfboard Barry could just ride into the shore. Or I could watch Barry fumble his way through the meeting and probably ruin his chances of selling the account. Typically, I chose the latter. True, it may cost Barry a sale but it was usually worth it because once a Rep stepped on this land mine, especially in front of a superior, it rarely happened again.

The Lack of Leadership land mine gets triggered when you show up in Mr. Whizbang's office without a clear plan of action. You just show up in his or her office and after the pleasantries are exchanged there is a very obvious moment when either you are going to lead the meeting or you aren't. If you don't step out first and take charge of the conversation then you do two things to yourself:

1. You put Mr. Whizbang in the awkward position of taking charge of the meeting that you proposed.

2. You demonstrate to Mr. Whizbang that you are an amateur.

This is a particularly deadly land mine. While it's hard enough to get an appointment with Mr. Whizbang, the real work begins while you are in his or her office. Many of Mr. Whizbang's opinions and impressions are going to be formed in that meeting and if those impressions reflect poorly on you and/ or your organization, getting back on the plus side with Mr. Whizbang is nearly impossible.

Keep this in mind when you sit down with Mr. Whizbang on a sales call, or a job interview, or any meeting of some importance: there is one question in the very front of Mr. Whizbang's mind and that is,

"Is this meeting going to be a waste of my time?"

How you conduct yourself at the very beginning of the meeting pretty much answers this question. The best way to answer the question is to take charge and lead the meeting. You will have a very difficult time leading the discussion without a plan of action. Taking the lead in a conversation should not be confused with ramming your agenda down Mr. Whizbang's throat. Taking the lead means stepping out

171

first with a suggested path of discussion. So lead. Respect-fully. Politely. But lead. Or at least make the attempt.

I say "make the attempt" because sometimes, and this is a very good sign when it happens, Mr. Whizbang will know what he or she wants to get out of the meeting and will assert himself or herself immediately.

I was doing some consulting work for a multimedia company when I got a call that they had just secured a meeting with the Mr. Whizbang of a Fortune 15 company. Breaking this account open could easily triple the multimedia company's revenue. So we worked out the presentation for the pitch meeting. We had charts, graphs, slides and handouts. So, safe to say, we had a plan. We knew what we wanted to communicate and we were prepared.

We got into the meeting and Mr. Whizbang was very polite as we began our presentation. But then five minutes into it, Mr. Whizbang spoke up:

Mr. Whizbang: "Marty, listen, I only have about fifteen minutes because I have to jump into another meeting. We have a bit of a situation here. My team is presenting in front of the Board of Directors in two weeks and we need some high-end graphics and animations done. Have you guys done anything like that recently?"

The multi-media company wound up doing the graphics and animations for Mr. Whizbang's Board Meeting. Mr. Whizbang then proceeded to hand the company nine more projects over the next four months.

When Mr. Whizbang wrests control of the meeting from you, it is usually a very good thing. At this point it is right and proper to follow his or her lead and keep your wits about you. You just caught a great wave; try not to fall off your surfboard.

But that's actually a rare occurrence. If you show up in Mr. Whizbang's office or conference room and, because you have no solid plan you do not take charge of the conversation or at least make a professional attempt at leading the discussion, you have just set off the Lack of Leadership land mine. In doing so, you have answered Mr. Whizbang's unspoken "waste of time" question with a resounding "Probably."

Avoiding the Lack of Leadership Land Mine

This land mine is not as easy to avoid as some others. Avoiding this one takes work.

Let's go back to the scene where I am sitting in a car with my sales rep on a beautiful sunny day, getting ready to walk into an appointment, and I say:

"Ok, give me an idea of what's going to go on in this meeting."

Sometimes the rep would not hesitate a beat and say something along the lines of:

"Well, I have their Web site printed out and so I want to make sure we discuss their West Coast distribution center. I think we can help these guys consolidate some of their overlapping functions..."

My confidence in the rep would go straight up. And usually, the well-prepared rep would be able to step out and easily lead the conversation once we got to sit down with Mr. Whizbang.

But no matter how well prepared they are, many of the same business professionals who are very adept at the small talk and words of welcome, business card exchange, and other rituals that begin this type of meeting, have a tough time making the transition to discussions about the business at hand.

If you are one of these people, the first step is recognizing that you have trouble with this part of a face-to-face meeting. The next step is to work on getting better. Because if you let this remain as a weakness you will always be in danger of setting off the Lack of Leadership land mine. No matter how good you are at setting appointments or getting job interviews, you'll always be starting out on faulty ground. Initiating this transition well is critical.

DEFINITION
initiate (transitive verb): to cause or facilitate the beginning of, to set going

---

Put another way, initiate means *you go first. You* be the one to turn the conversation to the business at hand. *You* be the one to lead. If Mr. Whizbang has other ideas for the meeting, he or she will let you know soon enough. But even in that situation, you should still beat Mr. Whizbang to initiating the material discussion.

Here are three useful expressions that, well placed, can help you initiate the transition from "Hey howdy" to "Ok, down to business."

1. "How long have you worked for (or owned) 123 Company?"

This question can be easily inserted once you feel the opening pleasantries and introductions have gone on long enough. It can also help steer a conversation that has been going along quite a while but still has nothing to do with business.

When you pose this question to Mr. Whizbang it will immediately begin to turn the conversation to the company. This question can help bridge the gap between the opening discussions and the discussions of a more material and productive nature.

I have never been refused an answer to this question and more often than not it is met with enthusiasm. In practical application, the exchange can go like this:

Mr. Whizbang: Good morning Marty.

Marty: Good morning Mr. Whizbang. Thanks for meeting with me today.

Mr. Whizbang: Sure thing.

Marty: (handing Mr. Whizbang my business card) Gary Blue tells me you are in his Rotary Club, is that true?

Mr. Whizbang: Oh sure. I've known Gary for about six years now. His kids and mine are in the same school so I see him all the time.

At this point I'm about ready to get down to business. I've always had a low threshold for small talk even though I know it is an essential business lubricant. Whatever your threshold for small talk is, it does not matter; just keep an eye on it. You'll know when you're ready to make the transition. That will be *before* Mr. Whizbang tires of the small talk ritual.

Marty: So you must know he and his wife have another one on the way.

Mr. Whizbang: Definitely. Due in February I think.

Marty: Yes, that's what I hear too. Tell me, I'm curious, how long have you worked here at 123 Company?

At this point we're easily off Gary Blue, the Rotary, and Gary's growing family. Mr. Whizbang is now telling me all about his or her entry into 123 Company and subsequent meteoric rise to power. I also will probably discover where Mr. Whizbang's been before his or her involvement in 123 Company. If Mr. Whizbang shares some personal history

175

then be careful! Getting mired in a lengthy discussion about how you've both worked in San Antonio can easily cause another unproductive delay. Do not fall into this trap. The key here is that Mr. Whizbang has begun talking about his or her relationship with 123 Company. Mr. Whizbang's talking about *business*. Now you can easily link right from that into the reasons why you thought a face-to-face meeting might do you both some professional good.

2. *"I was reading 123 Company's Website yesterday."*

This transition statement is a bit more abrupt but I have always found it very useful to kick a business meeting into gear. This statement assumes that you actually did read 123 Company's Web site at some point in the not too distant past.

This statement should be followed up by a relevant question that occurred to you while you paged through the Web site. If you have no question with which to follow up this statement, then this statement becomes a *non sequitur*. Spouting *non sequiturs* in Mr. Whizbang's office is not recommended. Assuming you have read the Web site and you have a relevant question or two, this can lead you directly down the path of discussions of substance. Here's an example:

Marty: So you must know he and his wife have another one on the way.

Mr. Whizbang: Definitely. Due in February I think.

Marty: Yes, that's what I hear too. Well, I was reading 123 Company's Web site yesterday and a question occurred to me that I was hoping you could answer.

Mr. Whizbang: I'll give it a try. Shoot.

Whammo, we've just departed Planet Small Talk. Now we can get into the process of doing some business or finding out if any business makes sense to do.

As a side note, keep in mind; it has been my experience that many times I have mentioned the company's Web site to someone within that company, and he or she immediately bemoans the poor state of their company's Internet presence. It is an absolute fact that an enormous amount of people genuinely despise their own Web sites.

That is why, while I encourage you to read the Web site of Mr. Whizbang's company, I also caution you against making any comment, no matter how sincere, about how much you like the site. It is very possible that Mr. Whizbang hates the site. He or she will appreciate your reading it, but think you are a moron if you overstate how great it is if he or she can't stand it.

3. *"Just curious, how much time did you have allotted for this meeting?"*

This is a great question because asking it has three distinct results - one direct, two indirect.

- ◆ Direct Result: Mr. Whizbang will tell you how much time he or she has allotted for the meeting, which is an excellent thing to know.
- ◆ Indirect Result: Mr. Whizbang will realize that you respect his or her time.
- ◆ Indirect Result: After Mr. Whizbang tells you how much time he or she has allotted for the meeting, a natural opening forms to move seamlessly from the small talk and engage Mr. Whizbang in a conversation of a more commercial nature.

This third transition technique is probably the most abrupt of the three. I use it all the time since it is an especially good question for Whizbangs who fall into the category of "Low Reactors." A Low Reactor is someone who is the opposite of chatty. The opposite of effusive. This person is tough to read and likes small talk even less than I do.

Mr. Whizbang will appreciate this question if he or she is indeed a Low Reactor because he or she will be relieved to get down to business quickly.

Mr. Whizbang: Good morning Marty.

Marty: Good morning Mr. Whizbang. Thanks for meeting with me today.

Mr. Whizbang: Sure thing.

Marty: (handing Mr. Whizbang my business card) Gary Blue tells me you are in his Rotary Club, is that true?

Mr. Whizbang: Yep.

Marty: I hear he and his wife have another one on the way.

Mr. Whizbang: Is that so.

Marty: That's what I hear. Before we begin, tell me, how much time have you allotted for this meeting?

Mr. Whizbang: I have a 3:30 conference call.

So now you know Mr. Whizbang is not one to yammer on endlessly with you about all things great and small. Mr. Whizbang is glad that you are getting down to business. It would probably be a poorly thought out plan to try and drag this type of Mr. Whizbang through the motions of extended small talk. He or she does not want to bond with you. Mr. Whizbang may want to do business with you or hire you.

But he or she is not about to be all folksy about it. Introducing one of those questions early in the conversation sets a very professional business tone that this type of Whizbang will appreciate.

Once you practice taking the lead in a face-to-face meeting with the Whizbangs out there, you will find your confidence growing. If you are having trouble making the transition from pleasantries to business, you may find the first few times you try a bit uncomfortable, but it will be well worth the effort. Once you start, you'll get better each time and then it will become second nature to you.

Bridging the conversational gap from small talk to business is *your* job. The Lack of Leadership land mine is one to be avoided at all costs. Mr. Whizbang is not looking to do business with or hire people who need to be led around.

Worth Repeating

❖ Many of Mr. Whizbang's opinions and impressions are going to be formed in a face-to-face meeting and if those impressions reflect poorly on you or your organization, getting back on the plus side with Mr. Whizbang is nearly impossible.

❖ The Lack of Leadership land mine gets triggered when you show up in Mr. Whizbang's office without a clear plan of action. After the pleasantries are exchanged there is a very obvious moment when either you are going to lead the meeting or you aren't.

❖ *You* be the one to turn the conversation to the business at hand. *You* be the one to lead. If Mr. Whizbang has other ideas for the meeting, he or she will let you know soon enough.

❖ Practice using transition statements to help bridge the conversational gap between pleasantries and business.

Super Words and Phrases of Immeasurable Power

"What Is The Best Possible Outcome of This Meeting/ E-Mail/ Phone Call?"

This is not a question that you ask of Mr. Whizbang. This is a question you should ask of *yourself.*

I learned this question from one of the very best sales reps I ever had the pleasure of supporting. For the purposes of this book her name was Jan. Jan was a very successful rep in Florida when I was working there. She was handed an account called Tiller Glass. Tiller Glass was a huge account but had been under contract with the competition for years. No matter, she made it a point to get to know everyone she could on Tiller's management team and gain a deep understanding of how, if ever she got the chance, her offering could benefit them.

Her shot came when Tiller Glass was bought by an Argentinean holding company who declared a review of all current vendor contracts. The playing field was leveled and Jan finally had an opportunity to sell the account.

She must have taken me to see people at Tiller Glass twelve times in the six months it took her to win the account. We also participated in an equal number of conference calls with various folks at Tiller and their new owners in Argentina. Even though some of the meetings were routine, Jan asked me this question before every customer interaction.

"What is the best possible outcome of this meeting?"

This question forced me into thinking about what we wanted from the interaction and making sure all our efforts, everything we said or did, drove us in the direction of our desired outcome. She asked me this so many times that I got used to having the answer ready well before she asked. I was always confident during my meetings with Tiller Glass because I always knew where we were going and how we were going to get there.

I incorporated Jan's question into my life as a sales manager. This question is an excellent one to pose to a rep when he or she pulls into the parking lot of an appointment or when he or she is getting ready to make an important call.

The answers I'd get were extremely telling. If a rep had been with me for a while, he or she would be expecting this question as I had come to expect it from Jan. But I always asked it anyway and I always had the rep tell me not only what the best possible outcome was, but also how we were going to get there from here. I did this because some reps, mostly newer reps, would have trouble gauging what was probable as an outcome. For instance, I remember sitting in the parking lot with a rep I'd unfortunately inherited from another sales team. For his own protection let's call him Pencil.

Marty: Pencil. My man. What is the best possible outcome of this meeting?

Pencil: (Searching under his car seat for a business card.) Gonna sell 'em!

Marty: Hm, excellent idea. However, seeing as how this is a $45,000 account and they've actually never met us, do you think they are going to make that kind of decision today?

Pencil: (looking at his teeth in the rearview mirror) Probably not.

Marty: Yes, so given that, what do you figure is the best possible outcome of this meeting?

Fortunately I have forgotten what Pencil's response was. I do remember that with every word he became more irritating and it was plain to see that the answer to the question was actually "I haven't given that much thought." Of course he did not sell that account and the appointment was a train wreck. What a waste of everyone's time.

The "What is the best possible outcome" question forces you into making the mental connections between the action (the call, the e-mail, the appointment) and the goal. Having helped you make those connections clearly, this question's ultimate value is in its ability to save you from wasting your own time. Many times, we get so caught up in the *actions* of business that the *goals* of these actions fall off our radar screen. This is dangerous because once the goals get forgotten, even temporarily, the connection between our actions and these goals is lost and time gets wasted. Your time and Mr. Whizbang's time.

I encourage you not to wait for someone else to ask you this question. I encourage you to ask it of yourself and hold yourself to having a well-thought out answer. Ask it before you pick up the phone, tap out an e-mail message, or leave for an appointment. Every time. Jan did and she now lives in a beach house the size of a grade school.

CHAPTER 16: Land Mine!

No Agreed-Upon Next Steps

I'm going to get to the big lie. But first, a universal truth. In the world of sales, having many appointments is the sign of an active and potentially successful sales person. Appointment activity is one of the most telling indicators of a winner.

In the world of job seekers, the same thing applies. You must get out there and go on as many interviews as you can if you want to get a job. Real estate agents will tell you the same thing when you are selling your house: if people consistently make appointments to see it, you can expect to get an offer. So it's true, for most business people appointments are what make the world go around.

But here's the big lie, business is NOT a numbers game. Sales and business success have a lot to do with mathematics. But it's NOT a numbers game. Business is a productivity game.

So many learned motivators, managers, trainers, and the like will tell you "It's a numbers game." I'm here to tell you it surely is NOT. It is true that having many appointments should lead to a proportionate number of sales, and as the number of appointments goes up, so should the number of sales. But that idea holds water ONLY if these appointments are productive.

If you are wondering whether you have conducted a productive face-to-face meeting, you have only to consider the Next Steps upon which you and Mr. Whizbang have agreed would take place.

Conducting face-to-face meetings without leaving with agreed-upon next steps is called "visiting." No one puts "Visitor" as their title on a business card, but you'd be surprised at how many professional Visitors there are out there.

This boggles my imagination. I know the task of getting face-to-face with Mr. Whizbang can be murder. And, if that's the case (and sometimes it is), why would anyone leave Mr. Whizbang's office without agreeing on some productive next steps? Incredibly, it happens all the time.

But what determines a next step? A "next step" is narrowly defined as a specific action with a committed completion date. Without both, all you have is a nice visit. The date is a key element of establishing agreement on next steps with Mr. Whizbang. It keeps him or her engaged in the process. So many times I've seen it happen. I'll be in a face-to-face meeting with a prospect and a rep. The conversation will be going great, synergies will be forming, partnerships will be leveraged, and we all leave with spirits running very high.

Then, days later, we wonder where all the love went. Somehow the enthusiasm died. The prospect has cooled off. How does this happen? Characteristically, this is what happens. We did not keep the client engaged with specific next steps. We never get back on Mr. Whizbang's calendar.

In the business world, Mr. Whizbang's calendar is easily the most important thing on Mr. Whizbang's desk. Sure, he or she will use a pen to sign the contract, give you the job, sign off on your raise, give you a promotion - but you won't have a chance to see Mr. Whizbang use that pen unless you get on his or her calendar.

So many folks break their backs getting into Mr. Whizbang's office only to walk out having wasted the opportunity to come back and move the process along. Let me illustrate.

I was in Columbia, South Carolina. Columbia! Home of the Gamecocks, the State Capital, and one of my favorite southern delicacies, shrimp and grits. Mmmmmm. I was visiting the sales office and was asked to accompany an excellent new sales rep named Tricia on an appointment. Tricia and I visited the owner of five independent bookstores. His name was Lars and he was a typical Mr. Whizbang. Lars wanted to network all his stores together with a data network. During the appointment Tricia did a great job of navigating through the client's wants and needs. She asked insightful questions and took lots of notes. But then, near the end of the meeting, the land mine went off.

Tricia: Ok Lars, is there anything else we need to cover?

Lars: I expect not. If we can hook everyone up at a reasonable price, we should be able to move forward.

Tricia: (Extending her arm to shake hands) Great! I'll follow up with you next week.

Lars: Super. Talk to you later.

Kaboom! The No Agreed-Upon Next Steps land mine just went off.

Nice visit, Trish. She had every opportunity in the world to have Lars agree to a few specific next steps with dates attached to them. She was right there. He was right there. Presumably his calendar was somewhere near there as well. She could have made it happen so easily. But she walked out without a single agreed-upon next step.

Now, let's split a few hairs here. True, she had next steps *in mind*. She was going to figure out his costs. She was going to produce a proposal. Then, once that was complete she would call and try to get another appointment. Even though she had the next steps in mind, they were not articulated in the appointment, agreed upon by Mr. Whizbang, or on his calendar somewhere. So therefore, by definition, she had only completed a "visit."

DEFINITION

agree (verb): a) to concur in (as an opinion); b) to consent to as a course of action

---

It does not matter if *you* have next steps in mind. It is only truly productive if you and Mr. Whizbang *agree* on the next steps. And assigning a date to each step you agree on is critical. Let me make some distinctions on what counts as a date and what does not:

"Call me next week." (Not a date)

"I get back into town on the 11th. We can get together then." (Not a date. This looks like a date but it isn't.)

"Call me Monday morning and we'll set something up for the afternoon." (Not a date.)

"I have the 21st at 2pm open. If that works for you we'll meet then." (Bingo! That is a date.)

The most common Next Steps to request are:

◆ Communicating answers to specific questions left open during the meeting;

◆ Second appointment to gather further information;

◆ Appointment to meet with others in the organization;

◆ Appointment to present the proposal and gain a decision.

Even beyond those, never leave Mr. Whizbang's office without reaching agreement on *some* next steps. It is hard enough to get in the door, don't shortchange yourself by triggering this land mine.

There is a covert advantage to keeping an eye on this land mine. If, for example, you have asked Mr. Whizbang to agree to some specific next steps with dates and times attached to them, sometimes Mr. Whizbang won't agree to commit to them. Watch out for this. When this happens, I always see it as a giant red flag. Mr. Whizbang's refusal to commit to some next steps, his or her skillful evasion of the issue even when it is presented plainly, presents several dilemmas:

◆ Mr. Whizbang already knows he or she is not going to buy from/hire you and is being purposely non-confrontational.

◆ Mr. Whizbang does not understand something about what you are trying to accomplish and does not want to appear stupid by asking you to explain.

◆ This person is actually not Mr. Whizbang even though he or she has presented him or herself as such.

If any of these scenarios is true, you can decide very quickly whether or not you want to invest any more time on the opportunity. That decision to stop investing the time in situations that are going nowhere is one of the secret hallmarks of very successful people. Very successful people have their personal radar tuned very keenly to detect when they are having their time wasted. They see Next Steps as homing devices – homing in on productivity and homing in on progress.

Avoiding the No Agreed-Upon Next Steps Land Mine

The best way to avoid this land mine is to have a decent idea of what the Next Steps are going to be *before* you walk into Mr. Whizbang's office. If you've done your research you should have a pretty good idea of what the appropriate Next Steps should be.

A case can be made that there are as many different Next Steps as there are fish in the sea. I tend to agree. However, as you move from appointment to appointment you will find that while every situation is a bit different, there are very few deviations from the standard *type* of Next Steps. Knowing that, it is very wise to try to anticipate some useful Next Steps prior to attending the meeting.

Keep in mind, every Next Step does not need to be your responsibility. In fact, one of the great litmus tests in business is whether or not Mr. Whizbang will perform a business action for you. When you give a Whizbang to whom you've never spoken a "To-Do" on voice-mail, you step on a land mine. In a face-to-face meeting, when you get Mr. Whizbang to agree on some business actions to perform for you, you've moved the process along.

To whatever business action Mr. Whizbang commits, it must be physical. For example, attending a meeting is a physical act, and as such it falls into the category of business action. Making a phone call to some other folks in his organization to set you up with a meeting is a physical act and as such it falls into the category of business action.

When I was a sales manager I would often ask a rep to debrief me on a particular appointment if I hadn't been able to attend myself. One of the questions I used to ask was "How did you leave it with the prospect? What are the Next Steps?" I would listen carefully to hear what actions *Mr. Whizbang* had agreed to perform. So many times all the

Next Steps would be the responsibility of the rep. Mr. Whizbang was nowhere to be found. I would encourage my reps, as I now encourage you, not to shy away from keeping Mr. Whizbang engaged by attributing the responsibility for a Next Step or two to him or her.

During the summary, when you ask Mr. Whizbang to agree to some specific Next Steps beware of the word "try." I want the word "try" to ring a serious bell every time you hear it. It has been my experience that this word does not bode well at all.

> *There is not try. Only do.*
> --Yoda

Master Yoda expresses my sentiments exactly. Don't try to set Next Steps. Set them. Diplomatically get Mr. Whizbang to help set them. But set them.

In order to illustrate my point further here is a quiz called "What Do They Really Mean?"

You: So, are you coming to my house tomorrow for the cook-out?

Them: Um, sure. We'll try to make it over there.

What Do They Really Mean?

Correct! They mean they have no intention of coming over. "Try?" As in, they are going to make an *attempt* to come over and they are just alerting you that they might get mysteriously thwarted in their efforts? I'm sorry but that's not cutting it. Try, is a lie. Try is a deceitful attempt to avoid making a decision, facing responsibility, or confronting an issue.

Or how about this one:

You: Mr. Whizbang, can we meet back here at 3pm on the 12th?

Mr. Whizbang: The 12th? Sure. I'll try to get you some time then.

I do not believe anyone with any social acumen would rate Mr. Whizbang's enthusiasm for this meeting to be very high. To the degree that Mr. Whizbang is enthusiastic about the Next Steps, so goes his or her enthusiasm for you and what you are proposing.

Usually during a face-to-face meeting the logical Next Steps surface themselves intermittently and it is a very wise idea to write them down as they do. Then when you feel the momentum of the conversation beginning to fade, or as you notice yourself approaching the end of the time to which Mr. Whizbang has allotted for the meeting, it is up to you to steer the conversation into a *summary* of these Next Steps. Through the summary you can gain agreement on the Next Steps from Mr. Whizbang. This is where the land mine usually goes off. If you do not summarize the Next Steps, all agreement to them becomes an assumption which undermines any real progress.

The Next Step summary is the most productive part of the meeting. Believe it. However, it has been my unfortunate experience to have been on both sides of the desk and watch the summary get skipped. I've done it and I've seen it done. I think most folks skip the summary either out of ignorance or laziness. In either case, skipping the summary is unprofessional. The land mine has gone off and your opportunity has been lost.

During the face-to-face meeting, through your discussions with Mr. Whizbang you have laid the foundation for a future business relationship. Making the transition from these discussions to agreeing on Next Steps through a summary is the responsibility of the person who called the meeting. Presumably, 95% of the time that person will be you. The following statement may be helpful in initiating the transition:

"Is there anything we've left out?

As a sales rep, I learned this simple interrogative. Once I did I rarely, if ever, triggered the No Agreed-Upon Next Steps land mine again. When you ask this question you will usually be met with the answer "I don't think so." It is at that point that the transition window has been opened for you. A logical conversational follow up to that exchange is "Great. Before I go I just want to make sure I'm not missing anything from my notes." From there the segue into the summary should be pretty natural. Here's how it can play out:

You: Is there anything we've left out?

Mr. Whizbang: I don't think so.

You: (looking at your notes) Great. Before I go I'd like to make sure I'm not missing anything from my notes.

Mr. Whizbang: That's fine.

You: Ok, I'm going to provide you an e-mail with a link to our customer web-portal. I'll provide a temporary password too.

Mr. Whizbang: Great.

You: I'll also get you an answer on the Pacific Rim question.

Mr. Whizbang: Right. I'll need that before you get me the Web stuff.

You: Got it. You were going to get me Mr. Healy's number so I can set up a meeting with him. Do you think you can get that to me today? I want to talk with him before the week is out.

Mr. Whizbang: No problem.

You: Excellent. Do you have your calendar handy?

Mr. Whizbang: Sure.

You: Will you please find a spot for me on your schedule on Tuesday the 18th? I have that whole day open."

Mr. Whizbang: I can give you about 45 minutes after 2:00.

You: Super. 2:00 it is. I'll present a brief review and then we can decide if it makes sense to move forward or not.

Mr. Whizbang: Great.

You've avoided the No Agreed-Upon Next Steps land mine. Now all you have to do is stand up, shake hands, and walk out with your head held high and your schedule intact.

By the way, without a summary, that conversation goes like this:

You: Is there anything we've left out?

Mr. Whizbang: I don't think so.

You: Great. Well, I'll follow up with you on all this and we can get together again next week.

Mr. Whizbang: Sounds great.

Clearly that is a weaker ending to the meeting. And I'm not proposing that without a summary no business gets done. But if a summary is easy to do and it can set you apart professionally, why not do it? Why end your meeting on a weak note when you can end on one of strength? Why set off the land mine? You are only a summary of Next Steps away from avoiding it.

Even though it is your responsibility to initiate the transition into agreeing on Next Steps, sometimes Mr. Whizbang will beat you to it with a quick "Ok, Marty, that sounds great. Here's what I think we ought to do going forward..." When Mr. Whizbang initiates the discussion of Next Steps, it is what we in sales call a buying sign. This is especially true in a job interview. If this happens, just follow Mr. Whizbang's nose. Ride that surfboard right in to the shore and be happy the Business Gods are smiling on you.

Worth Repeating

❖ Success is not a numbers game, it is a productivity game.

❖ Conducting face-to-face meetings without leaving with agreed-upon Next Steps is called "visiting." Visiting is not productive.

❖ A "next step" is narrowly defined as a specific action and a committed completion date.

❖ It does not matter if you have Next Steps in mind. It is only truly productive if you and Mr. Whizbang *agree* on the Next Steps.

❖ Every Next Step does not need to be your responsibility. In fact, one of the great litmus tests in business is whether or not Mr. Whizbang will perform a business action for you.

❖ Beware the word "try." "Try" is a lie. "Try" is a deceitful attempt to avoid making a decision, facing responsibility, or confronting an issue.

❖ The Next Step summary is the most productive part of a face-to-face meeting.

❖ If Mr. Whizbang initiates the discussion of Next Steps, it is a buying sign. Rejoice.

CHAPTER 17: Land Mine!

Lack of Insightful Questions

I remember it was early December when I found myself at my desk pondering my situation. It was only 4:30 in the afternoon but the sun had already gone down completely and because it was pitch black outside, I could see myself reflected in my window. Tomorrow was a big day.

I was staring down the barrel of a job interview and I was most unnerved. I had been working for the same company for about seven or eight years and even though I'd interviewed many times for various positions within the organization this was going to be an actual job interview. The first one in a very long time.

Before genuine panic took over I called my friend Dave. Luck was on my side as I found him at his desk. I'm sure he didn't know it, and of course neither did I, but through that conversation Dave imparted some very valuable wisdom to me that allowed me to avoid the Lack of Insightful Questions land mine.

Dave: So what's the problem? You'll do fine.

Marty: I know.

Dave: Did you read their Web site?

Marty: Absolutely.

Dave: Don't forget to close him for the job.

Marty: I know.

Dave: What questions are you going to ask him?

Marty: Questions? I hadn't given it much thought...
Is that bad?

Dave: Yeah, that's bad.

Dave went on to explain that in any given business meeting, especially a job interview, one of the things that separates the keepers from the sweepers was the caliber of their questions.

So that night of course I set about the task of assembling a list of insightful questions and had them at the ready when I sat down for the interview. Sure enough, during the course of the interview Mr. Whizbang asked me if I had any questions about the position or the company. I could feel my stock price rising in his mind as I started off with: "Yes. Actually I do. When I was reading your Web site, I was curious about..." That interview went very well and I took the job when they offered it to me.

Through that experience I had a chance to learn firsthand the value of having a few well-thought-out questions in hand before I went into a business situation of any gravity. And it is a fact that many times afterward when I was interviewing candidates myself I would always ask the candidate if they had any questions. Some candidates came right back at me with some thoughtful questions and that always made them more attractive as a hire. The topics of the questions, whether they were about the responsibilities of the position, benefits the company offered, me, compensation, or future advancement opportunities, did not really matter to me. As long as the questions were relevant, I was happy.

Then there were other candidates who did just fine in the interview until I'd hit them with, "Do you have any questions?" they would, for just a second stare blankly at me like I'd asked them to explain the Pythagorean Theorem[2]. Then they'd catch themselves and simply cough up an "Um, no, not really." I never saw the inability to ask good questions as a good sign in any candidate.

As important as good questions are in a job interview, they are absolutely *essential* in a sales scenario. When you are going to meet with Mr. Whizbang on a sales call, your questions are going to make or break you. Let me give you an example of a terrible sales call, in which I had the unfortunate occasion to be on the Whizbang side of the desk.

The sales rep, whom we shall call Trent, had seen me give a speech and approached me after the event. He represented Hubris Printing, a printing company that specialized in short-run production jobs. This was a fortunate coincidence, I told him, because we were almost finished with the design work on some specialized training materials and our regular printing company was giving us a hard time about printing only a few copies.

Ten days later Trent landed in my office. After the opening pleasantries, Trent gave me an excellent rundown of the capabilities and highlights of his company. Trent was doing fine. But then he started asking questions and the Lack of Insightful Questions land mine started going off all over the place. Here are a few examples:

---

[2]The Pythagorean Theorem states that $a2+b2=c2$. C represents the length of the hypotenuse of a triangle, while a and b represent the sides. This theorem is of fundamental importance in Euclidean geometry, where it serves as a basis for the definition of distance between two points. Or so I'm told.

Trent: "Well, Marty, tell me a little about your business."

I detest this question. It is my sincere belief that the Whizbangs of the world hate it too. This question annoys Mr. Whizbang because it implies that Trent doesn't know about Mr. Whizbang's business, and since the information is readily available, it shows or at least gives the appearance that Trent is unprepared or just dense.

Why would Trent assume that he had something of value to offer Mr. Whizbang's business if he doesn't know very much about it? Also, this question pressures Mr. Whizbang to start talking about a very wide subject without an idea of what specific information to provide. The parade of thoughts that roam through Mr. Whizbang's mind might look like this:

Do you want me to talk about the Company history? Do you want to know about our revenues? Do you want to hear about how the departments are structured? Do you want to know about my department specifically? Our product lines? My staff? What?

Usually, because questions like that are so vague, Mr. Whizbang is forced to ask "What do you want to know?" And then maybe the conversation takes a productive turn. But why even ask that question if Mr. Whizbang has to get you to clarify the question just so he or she can make the answer relevant to your discourse?

And now, back to Trent.

Trent: (smiling) "That's great. Tell me, what do you look for in a vendor?"

There is a little-known entry in the *Executive's Guide to Corporate Conduct* that states, and I'm paraphrasing here, "it is unwise, somewhat impolite, and almost certainly unlawful to throw heavy, sharp, or potentially toxic objects at a sales person even if they ask you a question like, 'What do you look for in a vendor?'"

At this point I am sorry I ever gave Trent an appointment. Had I known him to be this scripted, this vacuous, this unproductive, I might have saved him his time-wasting endeavor. But no, he masked himself behind a shield of professionalism, a Brooks Brothers suit and shiny shoes. So I took him on first impressions and I got burned.

The "What do you look for in a vendor" question has been touted to me by more than a few corporate trainers as being an excellent question to propose on a sales call. I bought it each time they sold it to me. But then, years later, I found myself on the Whizbang side of the desk, I discovered how patently low-rent this question is.

Go ahead, ask Mr. Whizbang this question. I dare you. I double dare you. I also double dare you to commission a custom made, self energizing neon sign to wear about your neck that blinks "I am an amateur!" Either way, Mr. Whizbang will get the picture quickly.

The problem with this question, even when it's asked with the best of intentions, is that you already know the answer. Everybody does. Mr. Whizbang is going to tell you he or she wants the following:

◆ Reliability
◆ Integrity
◆ Fair price

And that's about it. Mr. Whizbang may say a million things in answering this question but none will stray too far from those categories. I have never heard an inventive answer to this question. The reason for this is the question *itself* is as uninventive as it gets and reflects poorly on those with the ignorance to ask it. If I sound harsh, consider this: how harsh is an irretrievable business opportunity or a lost sale?

Trent was flying. He was in Mr. Whizbang's office and his tie was murder. I was wondering when we'd get to my short-run training materials problem. Could his company do it? How quickly could the project be turned around? How much would they charge me? Trent hit me with:

Trent: "Marty, if you had to make a decision today, would you go with Hubris Printing?"

"If you had to make a decision today?" I was absolutely dumbfounded. Trent was putting the trial close on me. I looked back at Trent and found I no longer hated him. I marveled at his ignorance and wondered how I could cut the meeting short without offending him. But I no longer hated him.

Here we were in a first appointment and Trent was putting a trial close on me. He hadn't even gotten any information about my particular project. He'd told me all about his company and his company's abilities. But he had no idea of what specific needs I had. This question is another one out of the widely published Sales 101 Book of Bad Questions. The real problem with this question is the "If you had to make a decision today" part is usually ham-handed and presumptuous. Worse, it backs Mr. Whizbang into a corner. I can assure you that this is not a position Mr. Whizbang enjoys. Asking this question is risky. Asking this question too soon in the sales process is the kiss of death.

I'm sure Hubris Printing could have done a fine job with the project but that is not important. What was important was that I definitely did not want to put that project in Trent's hands. No way. My appointment with Trent eventually ended and shortly thereafter I had another printing company handle our project. The reason was simple, this project was way too important and my experience with Trent left me with the impression that he was a rank amateur. I got this impression through the questions he asked me in my office. By the end of that appointment I was nearly deaf from the sound of exploding communication land mines. Clearly Trent hadn't prepared. He tried to "wing it."

I encourage you to remove the phrase "wing it" from your vocabulary. Consider these frightening exchanges:

You: Do you have a plan that you will follow when you build my new house?

Building Contractor: Nope. I'm gonna wing it.

You: What procedure will you follow while you perform my brain surgery?

Brain Surgeon: I don't know. I'm thinking I'm gonna wing it.

You: What recipes are you using when you cook for your new in-laws?

Newlywed: Um, whatever. I think I'm just going to wing it.

You: What plans do you have for investing my life savings?"

Your Broker: Don't worry, I'm just gonna wing it.

You: You must have prepared quite a bit to defend me in this lawsuit.

Your Lawyer: Not really. I'm probably just going to wing it.

Your Sales Manager: Ok, it took you six weeks to get this appointment. What are you going to ask Mr. Whizbang once we get in there?

You: Hadn't given it much thought. I suppose I'll just get in there and wing it.

One does not need to be Nostradamus to perceive that none of those answers bodes well for a successful outcome. Why then is the wing it answer so prevalent in the business world? The opposite of wing it is "follow my well-thought-out plan that I have outlined here on paper." Preparation is the best way to avoid the Lack of Insightful Questions land mine.

Remove "wing it" from your professional vocabulary and you'll be better off. If you wing it with Mr. Whizbang, he or she is going to know. You may think that you are crafty enough and seasoned enough that this does not apply to you. You may believe you can wing it in front of Mr. Whizbang and he or she will never know. But I think you are wrong.

Trying to execute any productive and compelling meeting with Mr. Whizbang without having gone through the process of developing some solid questions is like trying to write a decent book report having only read the back of the book. Your Lack of Preparation is eventually going to show, and when it does, the reflection on you will be rather poor. Stepping on this land mine quietly is impossible. The Lack of Insightful Questions land mine is a pretty loud one.

Nothing shows Mr. Whizbang how well or how poorly you've prepared for the meeting than the relevance and intelligence of your questions. Poor preparation generally leads to poor business encounters, and poor business encounters are usually the result of a Lack of Insightful Questions to stimulate the discussion.

Avoiding the Lack of Insightful Questions Land Mine

The questions you ask Mr. Whizbang are going to reveal your ignorance or your insight. My advice is to aspire to be categorized as having insight.

DEFINITION

insight (noun): a) the power or act of seeing into a situation; b) the act or result of apprehending the inner nature of things or of seeing intuitively

---

So, how do you go about generating insightful questions? How do we display that you've apprehended the inner nature of the situation?

The key is to make any question you have seem like it has been generated especially, *specifically* for Mr. Whizbang. Specifics are integral to customizing your questions. Your questions need to show Mr. Whizbang you've done your homework.

The *general nature* of the questions that you ask during face-to-face meetings with all of the Whizbangs you meet can be the same, but it is absolutely essential to customize the questions you ask Mr. Whizbang about his or her company, or what you know about his or her agenda. Let's turn a few of Trent's questions around so he avoids stepping on the Lack of Insightful Questions land mine.

BAD Trent: Well, Marty, tell me a little about your business.

GOOD Trent: Marty, I read the press release on your Web site that you are expanding the Training Department. I'm curious to know how the project we spoke about fits into your goals for that department's expansion.

Well now, sit back and let me tell you Trent, my boy.... And I'm off and running, telling Trent everything he needs to know about "my business." All he did was read a press release and then weave that right into a question that casts him in an entirely different light.

BAD Trent: Tell me, what do you look for in a vendor?

GOOD Trent: When I was preparing for this meeting I noticed that you chose Docu-Tech to design and deliver your on-line billing solution. What was it about them that made you chose them as your partner on that project?

Again, a little homework will allow you to demonstrate some insight into Mr. Whizbang's situation. Homework will go a very long way for you in front of Mr. Whizbang and you do not have to be afraid to mention it.

Phrases like:

- "While I was preparing for this meeting…"
- "I noticed when I was reading your press releases…"
- "Through my research on Whizbang Inc…"
- "I had a question come up while I was reading up on Whizbang Inc…"

are all acceptable in a meeting with Mr. Whizbang. If you've done your homework it is okay to show it. It is not okay to flaunt it. Using one of those phrases will be quite enough to get your point across. Using all of them would be, in my opinion, a bit obvious.

With this question, Trent is going to get the answer he wants about the things I look for in a vendor. He is going to get that and more. But the point is that the second, GOOD Trent version of the question is just a customization of the first version. The combination of homework and customization makes all the difference in demonstrating insight.

BAD Trent: Marty, if you had to make a decision today, would you go with Hubris Printing?

GOOD Trent: Marty, in regards to your short-run project, do you see any places where Hubris Printing would *not* be a tight fit?

This example assumes that Trent has already asked the proper questions to gain the information about the project.

In the second version of this question, Trent has not backed me into a corner, he's just asking my opinion. So I am much more disposed to answer him. This question has long been a favorite of mine because it is a very non-threatening way to ask "So, is there any reason we can't do business together?"

When Mr. Whizbang starts to answer this question, I encourage you to pay very close attention because he or she is about to tell you why you will not get the job, or the sale, or whatever it is you seek from him or her. Asked this way, this question tends to allow Mr. Whizbang to surface those often *hidden* objections and obstacles. In fact, I've often asked this question toward the end of what I was considering a very successful face-to-face meeting and unearthed some very important hidden obstacles that I would have never otherwise have known were there.

There are many excellent texts out there that can give you list after list of good questions to ask in a face-to-face meeting with Mr. Whizbang. I encourage you to find one and read it. But in their practical application, without your customization, these questions can often sound very canned and actually do you more harm than good.

Also, I cannot impress upon you enough the importance of writing down your questions. Keeping your questions in your head is a bit risky. And even if you have a photographic memory, you will be missing out on a very simple opportunity to send Mr. Whizbang a valuable message of respect.

Writing the questions down and then pulling them out in a face-to-face appointment sends that message of respect. Do not think for a second that Mr. Whizbang will not notice that you are very well-prepared and that you thought so much of this meeting that you took the time to write out your questions.

To this day, when I am meeting with a potential client I always write down my specific questions. Inevitably the following exchange or something like it will occur:

Prospect: Is there anything else I can tell you?

Marty: Actually yes. I got a hold of one of your brochures and I wrote down a few questions I had about...

The very fact that I took the time to do my homework and write down my questions so I wouldn't forget sends a priceless message of respect to my Mr. Whizbang. I am convinced this is a point of differentiation for me and I encourage you to make it a point of differentiation for yourself.

Worth Repeating

❖ In any given business meeting, especially a job interview, one of the things that often separates the keepers from the sweepers is the caliber of their questions. As important as good questions are in a job interview, they are absolutely essential in a sales scenario.

❖ Remove the phrase "wing it" from your professional vocabulary.

❖ Aspire to be categorized as having insight.

❖ Make any question you ask seem like it has been generated especially, specifically, for Mr. Whizbang. Specifics are integral to customizing your questions. Your questions need to show Mr. Whizbang you've done your homework.

❖ The combination of homework and customization makes all the difference in demonstrating insight.

❖ Write down your questions.

Super Words and Phrases of Immeasurable Power

The Name of Mr. Whizbang's Company vs. "You Guys"

Remove the phrase "You guys" from your professional vocabulary. Do whatever you have to do to get rid of it. Find a witch doctor. Perform an elaborate exorcism. Do whatever you have to do, but get rid of the words "You guys."

In every professional situation, even in casual conversations, whenever you *would* use the phrase "You guys" replace it with the name of Mr. Whizbang's company.

Let's make some comparisons.

> *"I was hoping I could get on your schedule and see if there was a way we could help you guys."*
>
> vs.
>
> *"I was hoping I could get on your schedule and see if there was a way we could help Whizbang Inc."*

> *"Can you give me a brief outline of what you guys do?"*
>
> vs.
>
> *"Can you give me a brief outline of what Whizbang Inc. does?"*

Clearly the second sentences just sound more polished. Using "You guys" degrades your interaction into a slovenly familiarity that is rarely appropriate.

"You guys" lacks class.

"You guys" lacks professional maturity.

"You guys" is strictly amateur.

And let me tell you it is *everywhere*. If you are telling yourself right now that this does not apply to you then you are either in the vast minority or you do it so much you no longer even notice it. My money is on the latter. It is an obvious peeve of mine and I still catch myself doing it. "You guys" is to the professionalism of your interactions as crabgrass is to your lawn. It's ugly and it has a way of sneaking in all the time so you have to be on the lookout for it always.

I have already stated that the sweetest sound to anyone's ear is their own name. I also believe that the *second* sweetest sound to Mr. Whizbang's ear is the sound of his or her own company's name. In my professional interactions I look for any and every way to say the name of my prospect's company. I want that name coming out of my mouth whenever possible because I believe it reflects well on me and because it has a very positive effect on Mr. Whizbang. Also, the alternative, you guys, is so sloppy that it is worth the extra effort to avoid saying.

CHAPTER 18: Land Mine!

Not Taking Notes

Of all the land mines that one could step on during a face-to-face meeting with Mr. Whizbang, this is the big kahuna. Without question, this is the big one. Better you should set the appointment and not show up at all than to sit there across from Mr. Whizbang and not take any notes. Many people think this land mine goes off very rarely. But they are mistaken because it has been my experience that it goes off all the time.

Before I get a nosebleed from the dizzying heights of my soapbox I'll admit when I was just starting out, I stepped on this land mine a few times. A very learned man, the man who gave me my first sales job, Victor, pointed this land mine out to me when he went out on a sales call with me.

Victor was my very first sales manager. His mentorship was a lucky break for me because Victor had the rare combination of being a born salesperson and being able to teach other people how to do it. I was very lucky the day I met Victor and convinced him to give me a sales job on his team.

However, the first time Victor went out with me for a day of sales appointments was an unlucky day. Actually, in hindsight it may not have been my unlucky day at all. In fact it turned out to be an extremely embarrassing--but valuable--experience. I remember it well to this day.

Early that morning I picked up Victor at his house and off we went. I had four appointments lined up that day. I was in my best suit, my shiniest shoes, and I'd gotten my car washed for the occasion.

That day we visited one chicken processing plant, two mushroom packaging centers, and finished up with a travel agency. I was flying. This was very early on in my career and by my very conservative estimate I was doing great.

As we drove home I expected Victor to tell me how impressed he was with me. To his credit he did praise me on the things I did well, but he had a more important point to make. As we were driving back to the office, Victor leaned over in the passenger seat and turned off the radio.

Victor: How do you think you did today?

Marty: Well, four appointments isn't too bad. I think those chicken guys were loving us. Probably close them this month.

Victor: This month? Hm, I admire your enthusiasm.

Marty: Thanks.

Victor: I also liked your interviewing skills. You really know how to get a prospect talking.

Marty: Yeah, well, you know it's usually a matter of…

Victor: (Pointing) See that drug store?

Marty: Um, what. Drug store?

Victor: Right over there. Get in the left lane.

Marty: Oh! Oh, yeah, no sweat.

We pulled up and parked.

Marty: You want me to wait here or…

Victor: No. You're coming with me. Turn the car off.

And in we went. My Spider-Sense was definitely tingling but I dismissed it as paranoia. I felt like we were playing hooky, walking around a drug store on business hours. But Victor was the boss, so I felt I was covered. However, my paranoia turned out to be right. Victor led me to the aisle that had racks and racks of office supplies. He bent over and picked up a single spiral notebook, turned and faced me.

Victor: Mart, you are pretty good and you could be great but let me tell you something. From what I saw today, I don't think you're going to last too much longer in this business and if things don't change I think you should start considering another line of work.

Marty: (Absolutely dumbfounded) Uh....

Victor: You wasted not only my entire day but about an hour of seven other people's day. You did more to damage our credibility in this territory in one day than I've seen in a long time.

(I stared at him with my mouth open. I must have made a noise, but if I did I can't remember it now.)

Victor: (Thrusting the spiral notebook into my hands) Know what one of these is?

(I couldn't put two syllables together. I just stood there staring, standing in the aisle of a drug store in my nice suit.)

Victor: (leaning toward me and fuming) It's a notebook, Mart. A notebook. See, you write stuff in it when prospects tell you stuff. Shows respect. And also, it helps you remember stuff. You went the whole day, the *whole day* without taking one single note in front of a prospect. I kept hoping you'd pull out a pen or a gum wrapper or something, *something*! But no, you simply wasted everybody's time. "

Marty: Victor, I'm sorry, I...

Victor: I don't really care. Look Mart, I want you on my team. Like I said, you could be great. But if you ever go on another appointment without taking notes, I'll fire you on the spot. Got it?

Marty: Got it.

Victor left me standing there, shocked and holding a spiral notebook in my hand. He went back to my car, and after I gained my composure I walked to the counter and bought the notebook. We drove back to the office in total silence. I didn't even have the nerve to put the radio on again.

Once I got back to my cubical I plopped myself down behind my desk. I was miserable. I didn't feel bad because I'd disappointed Victor. Disappointing him added to my misery. I didn't feel bad because I'd damaged my credibility with him and with my prospects. Lack of credibility is a frightening thing, of course. But that wasn't what upset me the most. I was mostly furious with myself because I had to be taught what seemed to me a very basic lesson. He hadn't taught me an esoteric sales technique, some hidden trick only the masters knew. No, this was a basic face-to-face meeting component. I thought I was Super Sales Guy, and he had to teach me Sales 101.

I never made that mistake again and Victor never fired me. In time Victor went his way and I went mine as so often happens in a big company. Many years later I ran into a guy who was also on that sales team. We reminisced about our old boss Victor. Curiosity got the best of me and I asked him

Marty: Hey, tell me, Victor ever take you to a drug store and like, show you a notebook?

Sales Guy: Drug store? No. Why?

Marty: Nothing.

Over time, I had come to believe the "drug store tactic" must have been something Victor did for all his new reps. But apparently he only did that for me. I always wondered why Victor singled me out for the drug store lesson. I guess he must have liked me.

I have been in my fair share of sales appointments sitting on the Whizbang side of the desk. I can tell you that a sales person or a job applicant that sits across the desk from me and fails to take any notes has their stock price fall every second they sit there.

I cannot begin to tell you how many times this happened. The worst times were when I'd have to remind a vendor constantly to write something down so they wouldn't forget to do it.

Here's a rule of thumb: If Mr. Whizbang ever asks you to write something down, you've already embarrassed yourself. For example, one of my instructions to a vendor went something like this:

Marty: Ok, so we have the first press release going out on Thursday the 11th, and that's the one about the new University contract. And if the paper picks it up we'll skip the Monday press release and we'll push it to that Wednesday which would be the... 17th. Now if we get stiffed by the press... here, you're going to want to write this down...

At this point I'm not happy. I have things I need to have happen and I have an extremely attentive rep in front of me who is not taking notes. My confidence in this person is not high. In the back of my mind I have two thoughts:

1. I must call this vendor and tell them to switch out my rep
2. I must remember to add the no-notes thing to my list. This drives me up a tree.

Mr. Whizbang does not need to see you transcribing your meeting with him or her word for word. But to sit there and not take *any* notes is inexcusable.

Taking notes says, "This is important enough to write down. This is something I want to remember." Also, it gives you an excellent resource at the end of a face-to-face meeting to access when you are recapping the meeting and setting a path forward. Not taking notes sends the exact opposite message and don't think Mr. Whizbang doesn't notice.

Avoiding the Not Taking Notes Land Mine

The short answer is, of course, take notes. Do that and you can't hurt yourself too badly. But let me give you two additional things to keep in mind as you avoid this very damaging land mine.

1. *Taking notes in the margin of your day planner does not count*

One of the most disturbing things I've experienced during my years on the Whizbang side of the desk was when a meeting with a vendor or a potential vendor would reach a point where actual business would be discussed and then suddenly the vendor would realize that taking notes would be a very good idea. Then, and this was the disturbing part, they would proceed to scribble down notes in the margin of their day planner.

Did they think I would not notice this? Is that how they keep important meeting notes organized? Did they think I'd just look the other way, that I would condone their lack of preparation?

I am not in favor of taking meeting notes in your day planner in general. I always felt the pages of a day planner were temporal, forgotten the minute the next day rolled around. Even if you have a huge 8.5 x 11 day planner, what happens if you need to take two pages of notes? And what if you have multiple appointments on the same day? Do all the meeting notes go on that page? Watching someone, a vendor, a potential vendor, or a job candidate take notes in their day planner never inspired a lot of confidence. I always preferred it when they'd use a plain notebook.

If you feel you must use your day planner as the repository for your meeting notes my advice is to buy the extra blank pages and take your notes back there.

What about a laptop?

Actually, I have only seen two sales reps fire up a laptop and use it for taking notes during a meeting. But I will say that I was impressed the few times I did see it. I asked one of the reps about it as the meeting was wrapping up and he said he used his contact management software to keep all his meeting notes in the right place. I was very pleased by this and I've often wondered why more folks don't do it.

What about a PDA?

My opinion on this one is, if you can master the art of taking notes on a PDA then more power to you. I am very pro-PDA, and even though I own one and travel with it I never use it for taking meeting notes. And I tried. I tried to get good at taking notes in that PDA shorthand but I never got fast enough to make taking notes with a pen and a notebook less effective.

2. *Take out your notebook* **before** *Mr. Whizbang says anything important*

If you are sitting across from Mr. Whizbang and while he's giving you some valuable information you have to duck into your briefcase and rummage around for your notebook, Mr. Whizbang is going to notice. He or she is going to notice because you just sent him or her three terrible messages about yourself:

1. You are not paying attention.
2. You are acting like an amateur.
3. It is possible you are in over your head.

None of these is a message you want to send to Mr. Whizbang but I assure you they get sent if you have to break out your notebook while he or she is in mid-sentence.

The easy way around this land mine is to make a habit of starting every meeting with a blank page in front of you. Spike used to do this without fail. When I interviewed with him, he sat across the table from me and before we started he took out a notebook, found the next blank page and put the date on top of it. He could have easily taken notes on my resume like everyone else did, but he used his notebook. I did not take much notice of it at the time but then a few days later I had my second interview with him and the president, Rex. Again, before we got rolling Spike took out his notebook, found the next blank page and put the date on top of it. This left an impression on me and ever since then I have done the same.

Taking notes sends a great message to Mr. Whizbang. It says you are prepared, you are taking this meeting seriously, you are a professional. It raises Mr. Whizbang's confidence in you and sets you apart from all the others who sit there and fail to take notes, or scramble for something on which to write when the idea to take a few notes occurs to them.

Worth Repeating

❖ Better you should set an appointment and not show up than to sit there in front of Mr. Whizbang and not take notes.

❖ If Mr. Whizbang asks you to write something down, you've embarrassed yourself.

❖ Taking notes in the margin of your day planner does not count.

❖ Be ready to take notes *before* Mr. Whizbang says anything important.

OK, What Next?

Well, let's begin by listing out the land mines themselves, just as a reminder:

The Phone

- ◆ Lack of Preparation
- ◆ Instant Launch
- ◆ Wrath of the Rep

Voice-mail

- ◆ Endless Message
- ◆ Phone Number at Mach Speed
- ◆ Calling Every Day
- ◆ Handing Out To-Do's

E-mail

- ◆ Term Paper
- ◆ Grammar and Spelling
- ◆ Emotional E-mail

Regular Mail

- ◆ Unsolicited Overnight
- ◆ Sanitary Mailer
- ◆ Metric Ton Mailer

Face to Face

- ◆ Dress Code
- ◆ Lack of Leadership
- ◆ No Agreed-Upon Next Steps
- ◆ Lack of Insightful Questions
- ◆ Not Taking Notes

I list them out here for a very specific reason. Now that you are familiar with what these landmines are, where they lie, and what kind of damage you can do to yourself when you trip one, you must keep them in front of you so you can make a habit of *avoiding* them. In your job search, your sales call, your college interview, whatever your endeavor your communication skills are going to be a major differentiator.

I would categorize myself as dumbfounded when I watch folks stumble on land mines time and time again. Unfortunately, some people jump up and down on land mines and negatively differentiate themselves. I don't know how you are going to feel when you watch a colleague self destruct on a communication land mine, but you are going to start noticing. What you do next is up to you.

Here's my quick assessment of what to do when you notice that a colleague has triggered a communication land mine, be it a member of your staff, a peer, or a superior.

Your Staff

If you have a staff, a team, a group working under you, or some sort of dotted line arrangement, it is part of your leadership responsibility to help your staff around as many land mines as possible. This certainly can lead to a scorching case of micromanagement and I advise you to avoid that at all costs. But when a member of your team has triggered or is about to trigger a land mine it is up to you as the team leader to point it out.

It may go without saying (but I am going to say it anyway) that this coaching needs to be done in private. When you are giving feedback to a member of your staff they are going to feel vulnerable no matter how well intentioned you are. The last thing that person needs is to have a potentially embarrassing action pointed out to them in front of an audience.

Even assuming the feedback is well-intentioned, well-thought out, and properly articulated, this exchange is going to test the maturity of the person on the receiving end. Keep an eye out for how your staff member reacts, and also keep this in mind when you are on the receiving end of some coaching from *your* superior. Your maturity will be tested and quite a bit will be said about you by the way you react.

When you are coaching a member of your team you might feel some tinge of hesitancy even if your intentions are good. It will be the same tinge of hesitancy you get when you notice someone has their fly open or possibly has a big piece of spinach caught in their teeth. If it were you you'd want that pointed out to you. And if you exhibit leadership behavior and point these land mines out to your team they will, if they have any sense at all, thank you for it.

Your Peers

What you do here depends entirely on your relationship with the individual. I will also add that in my experience it depends a lot on the gravity of the particular communication land mine itself. For example, if a peer tends to split their infinitives or is a tad abrupt on the phone I would probably just not mention it because these are minor.

On the other hand, if a peer is clearly and consistently damaging themselves in some form or fashion by the way they communicate. You may want to think about surfacing, delicately, the matter.

Your Superiors

You're on your own. I am not getting into this with you. Since 1991 I have had only two bosses who encouraged me to point out to them when they had tripped a land mine. Because of this, and of course many more reasons, these individuals still stand out in my mind as the best leaders and mentors I've ever had. These were very open minded leaders who checked their egos at the door when it meant they might learn something to improve themselves, or get an edge in some way. I only hope you have people like that come into your professional life.

In any case, the person who asserts him or herself best through written, voice, and face-to-face meetings will be the one who gets noticed. Your superior ability to communicate is your differentiator.

Your foresight, your insight, and your attention to detail are your friends. Cultivate them. Use them. Think! Pay attention. Plan. Do not be embarrassed to prepare. And whatever you do, keep these land mines in front of you and differentiate yourself by avoiding them. You *will* emerge as someone who really knows how to communicate with authority. Good luck. I'm rooting for you.

About the Author

Marty Clarke grew up in Oradell, New Jersey. He received his Bachelor's degree in English from Lafayette College in Easton, PA. His past experience in sales with MCI, where he won many national awards and became a sales instructor, along with his positions of Director of Business Products and VP of Marketing with BTI Telecommuniations proved to be an excellent training ground for Marty's current business: Martin Production, which focuses on corporate consulting, training program design and delivery, and speaking engagements. As a member of the National Speakers Association, Marty continues to draw enthusiastic audiences for his speeches and workshops, which include topics such as:

◆ Communication Land Mines: *18 Communication Catastrophes and How to Avoid Them*

◆ Headcount! *Waking Up From the Recruiting Nightmare*

◆ Company Man: *Lessons I've Learned from Working in Big Buildings*

◆ The Stand-Out Experience: *A Customer Service Strategy for the Real World*

Marty lives with his wife and 3 children in Raleigh, North Carolina. His interests include hockey, photography, and reading. However his passion for movies borders on obsessive and it's wise to stay away from the topic with him unless you have a lot of time.

To order books or to contract Marty for a speaking, training, or consulting engagement please visit:

www.martinproduction.com

9660 Falls of Neuse Road, Suite 138-233

Raleigh NC, 27615

919-518-0566

mclarke@martinproduction.com